THE SYSTEMS ENGINEER

Archives of Structured Chaos

By

Trace McQuaig

This book is dedicated to:

All the people who have helped me so much through life. Especially my family who have always been supportive and there for me. I've learned so much and can't wait to see what the future holds for all of us.

Table of Contents

Introduction

Congratulations on purchasing this book. I hope you enjoy reading it as much I did writing it all these years. You will find inside some of the daily thoughts from a Systems Engineer in the Information Technology world. Whether you are on a career path to becoming a Systems Engineer, a manager wanting to learn more about your employees, or a family or friend wanting to understand what your loved one does daily this book will open that world up to you. You will see how I thought about technology and business subjects. You will also see how my views progressed during the early days of Cloud technologies. Written by a seasoned technologist with over 20 years of experience. I maintain industry certifications such as CCDP, CCNP, TOGAF v9, ITIL v3 Foundation, MCSE: Messaging. You will find the insights of the Systems Engineering world to have something for everyone. What are you waiting for go to the next page!

CHAPTER 1: 2008, THE START

And it begins

Well folks. a thought is becoming reality here. I'm still customizing the site a bit as we get things rolling here. For now, you may want to just make a bookmark and come back in a few days.

Welcome! Allow me to introduce myself and the site

Well the site is customized about as much as I want it to be. For now. I may have gone a bit crazy with some ads. I'm interested to see if it is possible to still make money via web pages. Blogs are a new thing for me and I haven't been too hip lately. Although I am using blog software currently I may move to a different platform as this site develops.

Allow me to introduce myself. My name is Trace and I work for an Energy company in Information Technology. I am Manager of Infrastructure Systems. A bit of a fancy title for what I do. I 'manage' every single bit of gear except for desktops and handhelds. All network gear, servers, and phone systems. I leverage many new technologies to allow me to be able to do my job with little to no staff. The company is worth over $4 billion and has under 400 employees. I feel I am a hybrid between management and technical. Previously I was with a large mobile telephone carrier with over 80,000 employees. My range of experience has been in environments that were a small room with a few servers on a table to multiple sites with datacenters the size of a house.

I would like to let you all know what to expect here. First, I'll try to keep everything as G rated as possible so that you can read it from work. I have a vision of posting many technical snippets of information that will help others who arrive at problems I have already faced and solved or found solutions for. Let me say that they may not all even be technical. I also would like to begin building a social network of people who are in the field. Eventually I should have some links to either blogs or sites for other engineers and administrators. I may also end up talking about non-technical office issues and other items of interest as they pertain to information technology. In conclusion, I'm sure some views into my thought process and ideas will be here for the world as well.

I appreciate you stopping by and please check in from time to time.

VMWare Consolidated Backup and TSM

VCB is slowly evolving into a product I may feel safe using. Friday, I had a ticket opened with VMWare because I could not get VCB to correctly mount a virtual machines vmdk for backup. At first the problem looked to me as though vcb did not actually see the LUN. I double checked my SAN configurations and was confident it was a VMWare problem. One test we used was manually mounting the LUN with vcbmounter. When we started to use mountvm to see if we could mount the vmdk, someone in the background asked what backup agent and version we used. I told the engineer to tell them we used Tivoli Storage Manager 5.4.0.2.

The distant voice let us know that 5.5 was out and had some special support for vcb. I have had 5.5.0.0 deployed for some clients already and the server was currently running 5.5.0.0 as well. The distant voice came on the line and let me know how cool the support in 5.5.0.0 was. I had already begun taking over the WebEx session and installing the 5.5.0.0 client on the vcb server. He let me know of a problem where tsm baclient 5.5.0.0 and VCB 1.1.0.64559 do not automatically create the directories needed for mounting the lung. If you manually create the directories it will delete them when VCB cleans up, leaving you with no directories again for next backup. I found the fix for this issue, it's a maintenance release for 5.5.0.0. TSM baclient 5.5.0.4 is what you need to be upgraded to. This PDF talks about using VCB with Tivoli Storage Manager 5.5 check out page 329 in the document which is 347 of 402 in the pdf.

The APAR IC54709 is included as a fix in 5.5.0.4. You can download the patch here that will take you to 5.5.0.4.

A few features I feel are key:
1. The VCB server backs up the virtual machines using proxynode. This means that you can install an agent on the virtual machines and do file level restores as if they were backed up like normal.
2. License savings for TSM if your VCB server requires less licensing than your physical ESX servers.

Once you setup everything and create a vmlist file with all of your virtual machines. The only thing left is using a macro in your schedules to run "dsmc backup vm". The product seems to work pretty good after that. I'll try to test some restores next week and let you all know how that turns out. I'm very interested in keeping an eye on VCB as it develops, and I certainly appreciate the integration that Tivoli and VMWare are providing.

New Domain Name

Well I decided to go ahead and register a domain name for this site. After a few hours of brain storming and whois lookups I thought of this one. It was an instant hit with my friends and family. I hope it is easy enough for everyone to remember and catchy enough to survive the chaos most endure in my field before being able to get back to their bunker. Err...desk.

So, for now please update your bookmarks because I am here to stay!

Time Change. Spring

Have you ever asked yourself what time is it really? If you are IT, you may have heard of Network Time Protocol. NTP is very useful, as it allows devices to communicate with a central server or set of servers to keep their time synchronized. This usually works great. Some people have time servers in their infrastructure that keep time very accurately.

DST was changed in 2007 so that it comes several weeks earlier and ends several weeks later. March 9th, 2008 was the date for us here in the USA. Saturday night most of us set our clocks 1 hour ahead. If your infrastructure runs NTP servers and clients, you hopefully didn't have much to do. Our Cisco Call Managers require that we edit a field in the database to show the new change over dates which was edited in 2007 for us. However, they also require all the phones to be reset after each change over. This can easily be done by resetting all devices at the device pool level.

I'm not sure if it is related to the time change or not by my Citizen Skyhawk watch appears to have an issue. Now this watch is pretty darn cool. It uses radio signals from the atomic clock in Boulder, CO which broadcasts the WWVB time code. Every day at 4am my watch listens to these signals and sets its time. What a great feature you may say, and I agree. However, mine is not able to receive a signal at all right now. I've tried from my office which is on the 56th floor. I've tried from my home which is surrounded by concrete. It honestly usually works great from my home.

You may be thinking what does my watch have to do with any of this? Well I use the watch as a key way to tell if my NTP time settings on all my devices is correct. Normally the time on my NTP server and my watch are exact. At least as exact as my eyes and mind can tell. You can bet I'll be getting my watch repaired as soon as possible. Combining the accurate time with the always visible analog UTC time display my watch has and it is a valuable tool in the world of logs and troubleshooting.

I recommended you all take the time to see if your devices really think it is the same time you think it is... You may be surprised at what time it is at your company.

Negotiating with vendors. Here is how!

Have you ever brokered a deal for your company? Many companies have policies and budgets they are restricted by. When it comes time to purchase something the department needs or wants, how do you go about making sure you don't pay too much for it? If you have a budget it seems to only be in you and your department or company's best interest to find the best price. Sure, it would be great if every company gave you their best price up front, however this wouldn't make for good capitalism.

Please keep in mind I'm not suggesting this for small everyday items. I mean big projects, tens of thousands of dollars at a minimum. Sure, you can negotiate and broker a deal for smaller items but is it worth your time? It isn't worth my time. In my experience we try to keep at least three vendors that can supply us with the product we are looking for. If you have ever had to deal with multiple vendors and some of the random product numbers, skus, and packages just getting quotes that are comparable can be quite a task. For smaller items and projects, I would just stop right here with my 3 quotes and pick the lowest price.

It never seems to fail that vendors want to compete, and this is especially true on big ticket items. If your company doesn't have any policies against it, then why not facilitate this competition?

Let's set some rules to follow to ensure we don't cross any lines.

1. You should not personally profit in the form of cash.
2. You should not accept gifts (unless allowed by employer).
3. You should follow all your company polices.

Number one should be self-explanatory, any cash belongs to the company because you are not buying the product out of your pocket. Let's go over number two in some detail because I get asked about this a lot from co-workers. Now it is very common for vendors to take you and possibly co-workers to lunch for business meetings. This is fine with most, including me. However, you should also make sure it is ok with your company. This is a great way to build a relationship with your vendor. However, it can cause problems if you begin to feel obligated to the vendor. I would like to point out that it is in the vendors best interest to take you to lunch. The whole meal is tax deductible for the vendor company. They were going to pay the money in tax anyway so why not take a customer out to eat and talk business and/or put a smile on his or her face. These business lunches are an excellent way to discuss at a slightly higher view just about any business topic. It is also a great time to get the boss involved a bit. Everyone can give a little input on their experiences in the past and expectations for the future.

So now that we know where some of the lines are drawn we can get down to business.

Have your three vendors? Know what product you want? Get a quote from each vendor and make sure it is apples to apples. Take the lowest quote and let's say it is from vendor A. Now let's call the highest price vendor. Let's label them vendor B. Tell them that you want to see if they have any completive pricing available. This usually involves a call back where this vendor calls their distributor or finance department or some other person with approval authority for special pricing. If all goes well on their end you will get a much better price to "keep" your business. They usually expect to make it up in maintenance renewals. If they are unable to match or beat your lowest quote, then you need to tell them right there on the phone that they are higher. Usually they will ask where they need to be. I usually reply with the number they need to beat. This may be the exact value of my lowest quote or maybe even 1 or 2 percent less. If they can do it, they will send you a quote and they can stay in the competition. If they cannot, don't argue or waste any more time with them. They may try to explain how the provide value but usually this matters not. The bottom line is usually what is important.

Now it is time to call vendor A again. You play the same cards above. Ask them if they want to compete for your business as you have a quote that is lower. You can continue going back and forth here for some time depending on how aggressively the vendors are lowering their price. I have been amazed at how low some prices will go. I've even had vendors that were amazed at how low their competitors' prices would go. So much so that they would ask for the quote from their competitor. This is basically calling you a liar. Your quote is confidential. You should consider the pricing your vendors give you special. If you are asked for a quote for a vendor to lower their price this means they have their prices as low as they can go, and you do not need to negotiate with them any further. They are out of the race.

Let's assume vendor B was unable to beat vendor A's price. We simply start this process again with vendor C. You can even start the process with all your vendors at the same time. However, this can lead to communication issues. Eventually all your vendors will fall out of this competition as they reach their lowest price. I hope this helps you in your future business deals. It certainly has helped me in mine.

Troubleshooting VCB and TSM

Here are some commands that may be helpful. Unfortunately, VMWare's latest readme included in the latest Consolidated Backup integration Module VMware-ibm-tsm-integration-64559 does not talk about TSM 5.5 – only 5.3, 5.3.3, and 5.4. At the time of this writing, it does not look like TSM 5.5.0.4 is fully supporting full VM backups, only file level. I have reviewed this document from IBM on using VMWare Consolidated Backup with TSM 5.5 many times and cannot find any information on full VM backups. I expect a newer TSM integration module to be out soon, as this one was made in September 2007 where the info center document is from November 2007.

VMWare
Mounting:
To manually mount a VM's file system using vcbmounter use:
vcbmounter -h vcms.domain.com -u vcuser -p vcpass -a ipaddr:vmguest.domain.com -r c:\mnt\tsmvmbackup\filelevel -t file

To manually mount a VM for full backup use this instead
vcbmounter -h vcms.domain.com -u vcuser -p vcpass -a ipaddr:vmguest.domain.com -r c:\mnt\tsmvmbackup\fullvm -t fullvm

unmounting:
To unmount either use:
vcbmounter -h vcms.domain.com -u vcuser -p vcpass -U c:\mnt\tsmvmbackup\fullvm\vmguest
or
vcbmounter -h vcms.domain.com -u vcuser -p vcpass -U c:\mnt\tsmvmbackup\filelevel\vmguest

Tivoli
To manually start a backup using file level against a VM.
dsmc backup vm -vmlist=vmguest -vmchost=vcmserver -vmcuser=vcuser -vmcpw=vcpassword

The ability to offload your backups to a dedicated machine is great. Especially if you run your ESX servers as close to the edge as possible. I personally have a cluster with 38 virtual machines on 2 dell 2950's with 16 GB of ram each. I find myself assigning 512 MB of memory to a server and I will allow it more as I see fit.

TSM Operational Reporting - Review and Summary

Every morning I pick up my blackberry and look at an email from TSM Operational Reporting. If you are responsible for a Tivoli Storage Manager install you should be looking at a report from TSM Operational Reporting at some time during your day as well. TSMOR has two key reports that can be emailed to you. The daily and hourly reports work in tandem to give you a wide range of information when it is needed and focused information if there is ever a problem. In addition, TSMOR can store a current as well as previous reports, using html formatting, in a directory. Until TSMOR became available there was hardly any way to easily see the health of your TSM environment.

TSM Operational Reporting's daily report is about as complete of a report you can get. Beginning with a general summary of the target TSM server some of the items monitored are shown below.

These are simple counts or numbers:

Administrative Schedules – Success, Error, Fail, missed
Client Schedules – No error, skipped files, warnings, Errors, Failed, missed
Total GB – Backed up, Restored, Archived, retrieved
Database and Log utilization
DB Cache Hit Ratio
Diskpool Utilization
Scratch and Unavailable Volumes

Then it gives you some detailed information of the Administrative Schedules and Client Schedules. Detail such as what missed or failed. At this point I have a solid idea of the health and success of the previous backup cycle. From here I can move on to trouble-shooting problems if needed or can safely move on to other tasks if everything was successful. While scrolling down I pass up some awesome looking but often not useful for me graphs of different load summaries. I'll list them to see if any catch your attention.

Session Load Summary
Tape Mount Load Summary
Migration Load Summary
Reclamation Load Summary
Database Backup Load Summary
Storage Pool backup Load Summary
Expiration Load Summary

These graphs are useful for more of an 50,000 ft overview of the loads your server is under throughout the day. If I want a bit more detail on the clients such as Bytes Transferred or Node versions I can simply scroll down. The Node Activity Summary is one section I watch frequently. It gives a list of Nodes and their version of TSM BAClient. This is currently very useful in my environment as I am currently phasing out 5.3.x.x and moving to 5.5.0.4. Support for 5.3.x.x is not going to be available after April 30th, 2008.

The next section I have recently had to turn off. Activity Log Details is the output of your activity log for the past 24 hours. I have a few HSM for Windows clients and these have been generating a lot of information in the activity log. So much information in fact that it made my daily report fail. After disabling this section in the daily report, it runs just fine.

The Missed File Summary is useful at times. An example would be a new agent on all your machines that has a file that is being skipped on all the machines. You will see the number of occurrences of skipped files and the name of those files. The next section Missed File Details is what I use to troubleshoot missed files. It gives you two key pieces of information. The node name and the unc path to the file. The third piece of information is the time at which it was skipped. This time can be useful if you know some other job doesn't finish or start until a certain time to release the file. The first two pieces of information should give you enough information to know if you need to edit your include/excludes.

The Session Summary section is awesome. But mostly used for bragging. If you are a backup administrator, the only thing that comes close to being able to say you can and have restored anything is how fast you can do it. This section will list for each node:

Objects Inspected, Backed Up, Updated, Rebound, Failed
Bytes Moved
Elapsed Time
Aggregated Rate KB/Sec
Percent Compressed

If you are like me knowing how many objects and how fast they moved, and the total size of that data is a very good number to know. For instance, for nodes with lots of objects it may be worth it to have the Tivoli journal engine running. Slow aggregated Rate and high bytes moved can sometimes reveal network bottlenecks. Session Summary is available for both backup sessions and archive sessions as well as restores and retrieves. The last section is Timing Information which is how long it took in each section to gather the data.

I hope this review and summary has informed you a bit. There are many other features which I did not cover but may do so later. In case you would like to research them on your own I will point you in the right direction. You can create multiple daily and hourly reports. You can create your own custom select statements to pull data you need for your environment. You also can change any the parameters that cause the hourly report to notify you or show errors. One I change is number of scratch tapes required to be health from 5 to 3. I also have the hourly report only email me if there is a problem, such as out of scratch or a log filling up. You may also want to look at per node notifications which would be very handy in larger IT organizations where backups are done on servers you do not care about but someone else does.

Microsoft Enterprise Agreement SQL 2005 Install Gotcha!

If you have an Enterprise Agreement or Volume License from Microsoft, you may wish to bookmark this one. When downloading SQL 2005 Standard or Express you have 2 iso's to download. One has a #1 in the name and the other #2 in the name. Grab them both. The first is the servers install and the second is the tools. If you happen to only get the first, you will soon learn you cannot install the management consoles and other client connectivity options. Oh, sure the setup will allow you to select them. You'll even get the installation to kick off and run a bit. But rest assured by the time you get back from lunch your install will have failed. You'll see a message like:

> There was an unexpected failure during the setup wizard. You may review the setup logs and/or click the help button for more information.

You can go and double check your logs to make sure it is the same issue. Check the logs here:

> C:\Program Files\Microsoft SQL Server\90\Setup Bootstrap \LOG\Files

If it turns out to be the same issue you should see something like the following:

Running: InstallToolsAction.10 at: 2006/4/8 16:46:2
Error: Action "InstallToolsAction.10" threw an exception during execution.

Error information reported during run:

Target collection includes the local machine.

Fatal Exception caught while installing package: "10"

Error Code: 0x80070002 (2)
Windows Error Text: The system cannot find the file specified. Source File Name:

```
sqlchaining\sqlprereqpackagemutator.cpp
Compiler Timestamp: Tue Aug 9 01:14:20 2005
Function Name: sqls::SqlPreReqPackageMutator::modifyRequest
Source Line Number: 196
---- Context ------------------------------------------------
sqls::InstallPackageAction::perform
WinException caught while installing package. : 1603
Error Code: 0x80070643 (1603)
Windows Error Text: Fatal error during installation. Source File Name:
packageengine\installpackageaction.cpp
Compiler Timestamp: Fri Jul 1 01:28:25 2005
Function Name: sqls::InstallPackageAction::perform
Source Line Number: 167
---- Context ------------------------------------------------
sqls::InstallPackageAction::perform
```

If everything checks out this far then here is how to fix it. You need #1 and #2 iso's. Extract #1 to *:\sql2005\servers. Then extract #2 to *:\sql2005\tools. Now rerun your setup from the server's directory. Now when you select to install servers and client components etc. it will successfully install.

Source I used to fix my problem the first time.

http://support.microsoft.com/kb/916760/en-us

Vista, why are you so big?

Microsoft's recent desktop OS, and I call it desktop because I do not currently consider it a viable workstation OS, is almost 15GB installed. I'm currently running Vista on my workstation and laptop at the office. I also have it running on my home workstation. Before SP1 for Vista the windows directory was a whopping 14.9 GB in size. The largest directory was "winsxs" which apparently holds multiple versions of dll's and such used for compatibility. I have had many issues with Vista and was hoping SP1 would solve them all for me. Now that my windows directory is up to 20.1 GB with SP1 installed I'm disappointed to say that none of my issues were resolved.

Some current computer specifications are in order...

> Processor: Intel Q6600
> Memory: 4GB DDR2 PC8000
> Motherboard: ASUS P35
> Hard Drive: Raid0 SataII 200GB

As you can tell I do build my own home machines. At the office I have a Dell Precision T7400:

> Processor: Intel Xeon 5482
> Memory: 8GB DDR2
> Hard Drive: Raid0 SataII

Neither of these machines are what I would consider as under-powered. However, Vista always seems sluggish. At home I have a very annoying issue of just about anytime I open explorer the window is white and not responsive for about 30 seconds. After which it is perfectly fine. If you wait another 10 minutes to open explorer again then you will experience the same issue. At the office I have an issue with adding folders to my taskbar. I usually add the desktop to the task bar and use it as a menu system to quickly open items without having to minimize to the desktop. I'm fine up to this point, however once I lock my taskbar items a tiny bit of the first icon shows in the taskbar for the desktop. Unlock and it goes away. Very annoying.

Being a Systems Engineer usually means you get to manage some Microsoft products. One product I'm sure a lot of us get to manage is Exchange. If so you may have already found that you are unable to install the Microsoft Exchange Systems Management Console on Vista. It doesn't install with some missing features or say that it cannot be installed but still let you, it will not install, period. Another issue I found recently was that I must call Microsoft for a hotfix to get the DHCP admin working in Vista. How am I to manage all these Microsoft products when I cannot install the consoles or use the consoles on my workstations?

I was hoping SP1 would fix these issues that seem to bug me the most. However, after waiting the hour for SP1 to install on the 2 machines I use the most, I'm just about right where I was. Eventually I'm hoping Microsoft will get Vista running as good as XP. For now, I'll fight the urge to switch back to XP.

VMWare VCB and EMC PowerPath

VMware Consolidated Backup is going to continue to mature into a great solution for backing up VM's. Some of the early adopters may have experienced problems with centralized storage. If you have more than one path to your centralized storage it has been recommended in VMWare's documentation that you disable all inactive paths. This to me does not seem acceptable as part of the reason you paid for your highly available storage was for it to be "HIGHLY AVAILABLE". This was a big issue for me.

VMWare VCB 1.1.0 apparently works fine with PowerPath. I have configured this, and I am currently backing up about 20 guests. I am using Windows 2003 SP2 and PowerPath 5.1.0. The version of VCB I am using is exactly VMware-vcb-64559. I am also using Tivoli Storage Manager 5.5.0.4

I am unsure if VCB and PowerPath are officially supported yet. I am unable to find any documentation on VMWare's site that says it is supported. I am also unable to find anything in release notes or the forums. It was recommended to me by VMware support to see if it resolved a disk access issue we seemed to randomly be having. I'm happy to say that after installing PowerPath I can backup all my VM's I have in vmlist so far. I would try it in a lab environment for a bit. I'd be interested to hear if it works for anyone else.

Creative goes after driver Modder Daniel Kawakami

I have been a long-time user of Creative Labs SoundBlaster line of sound cards. I am currently running an X-Fi MusicExtreme on Vista x64. Many users who have SoundBlaster sound cards have only basic functionality on windows Vista. An individual, Daniel Kawakami, on the creative forums had modded the creative drivers to work perfectly on vista. He had enabled many of the features that apparently Creative disabled on purpose.

For Audigy owners he had successfully provided working drivers for things like the equalizer, CMSS, DVD audio, Dolby/DTS encoding and hardware midi in windows Vista. These features are available in XP. He simply made them work in Vista. Many think Creative disabled these features to force end users to upgrade. The Vista Audigy support pack was removed from creatives forums. Within 24 hours the community was outraged by their actions towards Daniel.

Here is a list of the forum's posts from Daniel with support packs. The files are property of Creative Labs.

> SB Live! for Vista
> Audigy for Vista
> Gameport for Vista

Here are direct links to the support packs at filefront.

> SB Live! for Vista
> Audigy for Vista
> Gameport for Vista

I will try to keep these updated as the posts are restored to creative's forums or I find them else ware. If I am officially contacted by Creative I may be forced to remove my links. I'm sure they will be gone from filefront by that time as well.

Creative had an official statement to Daniel Kawakami released by the VP Corporate Communications, Phil O'Shaughnessy. In this statement creative threatens legal action against Daniel. They also forbid him to accept donations for his work.

The bad publicity creative is getting for this won't soon be forgotten. They are quickly changing their statements, possibly already feeling the effect the community has. Many suggest they give Daniel a position at creative. I doubt he would accept after the way they have treated him so far.

Does Information Technology affect the stock price?

Does Information Technology affect the stock price? If zero help desk issues were to occur would the stock price of your company go up? If you have a catastrophic system failure event in your infrastructure would the stock price go down?

Obviously if your company is involved in e-commerce or some other high-tech public facing business then publicly visible downtime affects your ability to make money for the duration of the outage. I fully believe that your stock price is affected by the technology that provides your money-making ability. Your company likely has many polices and systems in place to minimize, if not remove, the risk of downtime all together. In this example I think it is safe to say that without a doubt e-commerce or your technology that is public facing affects your stock price.

What about the other companies? Let's look at an oil exploration company for instance. They likely only have a generic website. No other public facing technology. Let's say they have a major system outage for email. No email in the whole company for 24 hours. Do you think their stock price will be affected? How much will it be affected? If it was affected, let's say 0.1%, will it recover after email is working again?

What about email viruses and spam? Does the time lost to employees finding good email in the pile of spam amount to anything on the stock market? How about an executive not having a computer that works for a day or two? How about if an executive's phone fails to function for a day? And if his mobile phone fails? What if any of it was down for a week?

What if the company never had the technology? Are they not able to realize their full earning potential? I have vendors trying to sell me on technology all the time based on how much more efficient my company could be. If we are more efficient then wouldn't we be less efficient when the technology fails? Does more efficient mean higher stock prices? Does technology provide efficiency or convenience?

I would love to think that all the hard work that I put into my company's infrastructure systems somehow makes for a better stock price. In the end I think it all comes down to what your company does. It also depends on when that system outage occurs. So where do you invest in redundancy and fault tolerance? In your convenience's or your efficiency? Who makes the decisions on what is redundant and what is not at your company? If you made the decisions yourself did you do so with any input from your executive management?

More and more as technology is evolving in the workplace I have found the number one system is E-Mail. As unified communications become more popular I think we will find that communications in general is the single most important system for most companies. Ask around and let me know what is important at your company!

Farewell, Daniel Kawakami

After the Creative/Daniel K. fiasco, Daniel has decided to move on from modifying creative drivers for the public. This is likely the best choice for him and I do not blame him for choosing this path.

I'm sure many Creative customers would prefer to continue to get updated support packs. Daniel has posted a goodbye message on the Creative forums.

Daniel says:

"Although I still have my doubts, they've said I would not be threatened if I provided patches instead of the actual binaries, because of licensed technologies built into them (Dolby/DTS).
While this could even be true, most of the disabled features are Creative's own technologies, which means they've disabled them on their own choice.

Daniel goes on to say:
They were after me and, on a chat session, they asked me what I'd like from them, as if I were expecting something.
They've promised me a free X-Fi 2, but I told them it was not necessary, because I was getting a couple of cards from other companies that contacted me.
Well, at least they are getting flammed all over the web and they are certainly mad about it and I could feel it while chatting with them. That is an enough reward for my hard work."

In the goodbye post Daniel has put links to his forum posts with the driver support packs. I'm going to go ahead and link to the filefront pages as well as post the file hashes.
SB Audigy series Vista Support Pack v2.15.0004EQ with Equalizer (02/24/2008)
Download from Filefront
File hashes:
– CRC32: C99B3CF8
– MD5: 133B743BAAFADD9D681C56B0A0E0DEF2
– SHA1: D8C979C6E1BED6C3C3AB1C6FB425AD417D74A09C

SB Live! series Vista Support Pack 2.10.0001A (03/07/2008)
Download from Filefront
File hashes:
– CRC32: 15AFA064
– MD5: BBED0409A6941767ED263634B7A420EC
– SHA1: B84E8E37DDA0504204DA79AA8B8B585FD37D8461

Gameport support pack for Vista 32-bit (x86), updated on 02/01/2008

Download from Filefront
File Hashes:
– CRC32: 44585B0B
– MD5: F52B755900825968C4F5687CBA0E4C08
– SHA1: 9C4D1016DD79570F5BCA56C9A651148883532271

SB Audigy Value/SE/LS & Live! 24-bit Windows Vista Pack
1.04.0077B (02/06/2008)
Download from Filefront.
File Hashes:
– CRC32: 2218C974
– MD5: 3087EBB1C27F0DE19459F9FEECA1E7B7
– SHA1: 6C95377A0777D39ADC99193A43D43B2F764E68DD

SB X-Fi Xtreme Audio Windows Vista Pack 1.04.0078A
(02/06/2008)
Download from Filefront.
File Hashes:
– CRC32: 837372DB
– MD5: 0FF904877BA557E8E4DDBBE04F89EDEA
– SHA1: A2CF2FFF4816DBBC005A24D4E5E6BBA89A12AD05

Hopefully the above links will survive the test of time. I have stored the above files safely but do not have the bandwidth to host them. Should the filefront links fail I will find mirrors.

Daniel, I wish you the best. Publicity like this doesn't come every day, I would not blame you a bit for exploiting it a bit to get your foot in the door at Creative or a competitor if that is what you want to do. Who knows, you may be very happy with your current employment. I can't help but wonder if your PayPal account is tipping the scales with donations...

Good Luck Daniel!

UPDATE: 07.01.08

Well it looks like Daniel has edited some of his original posts. The drivers are also no longer on filefront. I have found an alternate location here.

Altiris Helpdesk Solution - Incidents via Email

When working with Altiris Helpdesk Solution be careful not to associate an email address of one of your users or workers with a queue. If you do this when that person sends in an email to create an incident it will generate an incident with no contact information. I have suggested to Altiris that they trust workers and contacts over queues by default. Here is a simple sql query you can use if you think you are running into this problem for an email address.

```
select * from contact
where email = 'emailalias@company.com'
```

If you get more than 1 result back you will experience the issue.

GFi MailEssentials AntiSpam Whitepaper

Spammers are not getting more creative and are using common file formats as attachments for pump-and-dump scams. This new white paper from GFI Software explains what makes spam such an unbearable problem and how spammers have switched from image spam to using PDF, Excel and ZIP file attachments. The white paper is free to download, and no registration is required for access!

GFi is a software company that has been around since before my IT career started. The white paper describes the recent tactics by spammers over the past few years. Attachment spam has been what I have seen the most lately. Spam is a problem for most of us, well, just about anyone with an email address. PDF spam is very annoying as it requires you to open a program to view your spam. Image spam is the lesser of the evil's as it usually will open in your mail client. Both spam types continue to plague mail systems taking up bandwidth and storage space. One problem that can quickly get out of control is the space required to store spam. If you allow spam into your mail system, chances are, your users are not deleting it. When you start to consider that up to 90% of your incoming mail could be spam, you quickly can see a problem. If you could reduce spam or even eliminate it your backups and mail storage would certainly feel the relief.

In my environment, I am storing one terabyte of email on disk. I am confident that this is valid email text and attachments. Imagine if I were not filtering the spam out. First my users would complain all the time. The managers would complain about their employee's lost productivity time from manually cleaning spam, if they were kind enough to clean the spam. I would also be storing 10 terabytes in my mail storage system. Spam filtering is a must have. If your company is new, then spam may not be a problem yet. If your company is an older company, you likely have already felt the sting of spam. In either case, allowing spam a way into your mail system is never a good idea.

Does music help keep you on task?

My line of work seems to drag me in many directions at once. One of the biggest challenges I face daily is staying on task. People seem to be one of my main distractions followed by computer distractions such as web browsing, email, and IM. I love answering people's questions via IM and Email but sometimes I must close the clients. At home this is fine, but in the office, I need to remain reachable, so the clients cannot be closed. To stay focused I seem to always rely on music I like.

I've been lucky so far that my companies have always allowed me to listen to music I enjoy. I've also been lucky to have ended up with nice speakers at the companies within a few months. Keeping the volume at a level that does not disturb others and trying to make sure that there are no questionable lyrics has ensured I stay under the radar. For the past few years I have also been making use of closed ear headphones.

Headphones seem to really be a great way to block out the office noise and replace it with some of my own. This works great for creating a work environment that is quite productive and allows me to stay in the zone for hours on end. Staying focused on what I am doing becomes a breeze and my mind doesn't seem to wander around everything that is happening.

I listen to mostly electronic music. This broad genre contains many different styles with various tempos. This makes it extremely easy to have music playing that fits the task. If I'm on a roll and knocking things out I can listen to some fast-paced beats. If I'm moving slow and working on something delicate I can listen to some slow paced chillout or triphop music.

I've recently purchased some new Ultrasone HFI-780 closed headphones. These sound great so far. Next time you find yourself not being able focus, try some music. If you already listen to music to stay focused, I'm always looking for new music.

Be careful with Altiris Helpdesk Tasks

I have been wanting to make a task that would force a notify rule to be enabled on a helpdesk incident. I wrote a set of queries and found what I needed to update. Once I created the task I stumbled across an issue. It has to do with Altiris HD solution processing the a sql statement before I even run the task.

My task looks a bit like this. It sets the workitem to have a rule '293' enabled on it.

```
Set: HDQUERY[[select workitem_number from dbo.workitem_wuci_join where workitem_wuci_join.wuci_id = '293' and workitem_wuci_join.workitem_number = WORKITEM(workitem_number)]]
```

The above is just filler really. The code that matters is below. Since Altiris doesn't provide a way to just update/insert a sql value you hide the sql statement in an HDQUERY macro.

To: HDQUERY[[select NULL insert into dbo.workitem_wuci_join (workitem_number, wuci_id) values (WORKITEM(workitem_number), 293)]]

However, each time the rule is displayed it updates the database. I think Altiris is processing the to: to get a value which is running the insert.

I also found that the select NULL was needed to suppress errors when running the rule. When running this rule, I found that it adds a duplicate entry for the 293 rule. This breaks the incident. To fix this use a sql delete in the workitem_wuci_join table of the altiris_incidents database.

delete * where workitem_number = '' and wuci_id = '293'

This will delete all rows (likely only 2) with the rule id and the incident number. Then you can simply edit the incident in help-desk console and add the proper notify rules.

Virtual Machine File System - VMFS

I was asked a question today and I thought it might be a good idea to begin posting the answers to some of the questions I am asked.

What is VMFS?

VMFS is Virtual Machine File System. It's just the file system that exists on the VMWare ESX servers.
In it exists files one of which is vmdk, virtual machine disk.
The is the VM guest itself. Instead of the virtual machines having a hard drive they have a vmdk.
All of the vmdk's are contained on a vmfs. Vmfs, ntfs, fat, fat32 these are all file systems.

EMC World 2008 - Las Vegas

I'm at EMC World 2008 is fabulous Las Vegas! I attended some really good sessions. Keep an eye out for interesting information I found as it will be posted here.

Cisco Live

Well I just got back from Cisco Networkers. It was held in Orlando, FL this year. It was an excellent conference with over 10,000 attendees. I took and passed 642-892 CCNP Composite as well as 642-873 Designing Cisco Network Service Architecture. This gives me Cisco Certified Design Professional.

I was ecstatic when I passed 642-873. Exams are half price at Networkers and I figured I would check this exam out. I had read the 642-871 book and felt I had enough knowledge to give it an honest effort. I'll be taking 642-825 and 642-845 in the near future to complete my CCNP. Next is either CCVP or possibly CCDE.

I managed to make it to some excellent sessions this year. One of which I was able to answer some questions for the session as well as get a book about ASA's for free from the presenter.

AT&T Managed Internet Tech Support

While troubleshooting a problem with circuits provided by AT&T I've had to deal with several people. If I end up building a simple tech support relationship after a few hours I sometimes ask where in the world the tech is. I also sometimes will ask if I don't recognize as accent or if I think I do know the accent and want to verify it.

In some cases, though, I ask out of frustration. Frustration caused by not being able to understand the person because English is not their first language. Today was one of those days. The support person was from Singapore. I was troubleshooting errors on a T1 circuit that was provided to a city in Arkansas. This trouble-shooting was being performed in the middle of the day. The office had been running on the backup circuit so intrusively testing the main circuit was ok.

Now I work with vendors a lot. I realize that it is cheaper to provide around the clock support by using call centers in other parts of the world during prime times. By doing this you can have employees working ~8am to ~5pm local times. I am ok with this. However, if it is 1pm Central Standard Time. Why am I speaking to Singapore? Is there no one in the United States of America who can troubleshoot a T1 circuit?

ATT, why am I speaking to Mr. Gonzales in Singapore? To add to the situation, we are talking over each other because of the lagged-out voice call. It feels like we need to say "over" each time we complete a statement.

From what I can gather Tier1 is in India or Pakistan. and Tier2 is in Singapore. There is a tier3, but you can only talk to them if ATT manages the router. I know the implementation and designer guys are in the USA. New York, I believe. So, setting up the circuits I get to speak to people in the USA. For everything else I am having to deal with Singapore and India. For what I pay, I want someone in the USA during business hours of 8am-5pm Central.

Telco - Clear to the smart jack!

While recently troubleshooting a T1 circuit issue for a MPLS connection I was getting the run around from my service provider. The classic phrase we have all heard. "Cleared on Test", "Clear to the smart jack", and "Testing clean on loop" as well as other variations are common phrases I hear. Telco is all too quick to dismiss my complaints and they always think they have no issues.

What if I am testing clean on loop? What if I am clearing on test? Who do we point the finger to then?

Well that is exactly what I had happen to me. Telco never saw the input and crc errors that I was getting on my serial interface. They could loop smart jack telco facing and test clean for all patterns. 0x1111 was giving me the most trouble. I could put my gear in hardware loop and send 0x1111 all day long just fine. But when I was connected to telco I would get about a 28% success rate. I knew it would be a cabling or telco issue. So, I changed the patch cable between smart jack and CSU. After the 3rd patch cable the issue remained.

Telco stuck to their guns telling me to change the cable. Finally, after getting telco and the various local exchange carriers on the line at the same time, with the backing of my hardware vendor I was able to find the issue. I had them loop customer facing from "test point" which happened to be on the telco side of the smart jack, about 60 miles from my gear. Somewhere in these 60 miles was an issue. I was determined to find it.

I asked telco to loop the smart jack customer facing. They couldn't do this. How convenient that they can loop telco facing to prove it isn't their issue but cannot loop customer facing to prove the customer doesn't have a problem. So, I did the next best thing. I had them put a coupler on the end of my patch cable before it plugs into the smart jack. I then was able to test clean on all test patterns, 0x1111 included. This ruled out my patch cable and my gear.

The LEC who was onsite assisting this troubleshooting happened to have a smart jack. I asked that he install it, so we could rule out the smart jack. I had the telco in the major city close to this office give me a loop customer facing from the test point. Sent my test patterns and tested clean!!! It was a telco issue, Imagine that. A bad smart jack. The kicker was the smart jack had been changed 4 days before hand in attempt to resolve the errors. Bad batch of smart jacks possibly.

So, the next time the telco has you running around to prove it isn't you. Stick to YOUR guns. Clear to smart jack doesn't always rule them out!

My BIG list of useful TSM commands and SQL queries

A quick way to find nodes that are not in a collocation group and how much data they are using up. I one onsite stgpool that uses collocation so I specify that I only want to look at data in that stg-pool.
select nod.node_name, nod.collocgroup_name, sum(oc.physical_mb/1024) as GB from nodes nod, occupancy oc where nod.node_name=oc.node_name and oc.stgpool_name='MYSTGPOOL' group by nod.node_name, nod.collocgroup_name

This is how I find out what tapes I need to move data off after running the above query and if I define nodes into a collocation group when they previous where not in one. This was I can reclaim tapes immediately rather than waiting for data to expire off the tape and space reclamation to run against the tape.
select distinct volume_name from volumeusage where node_name IN ('NODE1', 'NODE2', 'NODEX') and stgpool_name='MYSTGPOOL'

I hope to update this list as I think of other selects I use often.

VMworld

VMworld 2008 in fabulous Las Vegas!

It took a bit of work to get here as my home city was hit by Hurricane Ike the weekend I was scheduled to fly out to VMworld 2008 in Vegas.

Lots of contests going on. I have one from cibra where I need to match a card with someone else. If I can find the matching person, we win $300. Here is a picture of my card..

All paid attendees will have access to the pdfs for the sessions as well as flash videos. The videos are going to be audio over slides. These will be available by October 2008.

A new site has been launched by VMware. http://viops.vmware.com. This site is going to save us! It is a collection of best operational practices. It is in a discussion forum format.

I'll keep updating this post with useful information as I find it.

Virtually anything is possible.

Symantec Altiris Software Delivery Solution License Trouble

I have been fighting with Symantec Altiris Software Delivery Solution licenses for some time now. I have had numerous support calls trying to get Altiris to assist me in tracking down where each of these licenses has went. Today I found what I was looking for after Symantec Altiris support was unable to help me. I was told that they would not help me find a list of machines that were taking up licenses. I was unhappy about this and will reconsider my options going forward. I did submit a feature request to them. I just want to be able to prove that each license is being used up by a machine that I approve. In SWD 7.0 they are changing the license model to be based on agent installation. The current version I am using is 6.0 SP3.

Here is a SQL statement I captured using sql profiler that they execute to generate the number of in use Software Delivery Licenses.

exec sp_executesql N'SELECT COUNT(DISTINCT Stat.WrkstaId) FROM AeXEvt_AeX_SWD_Status as Stat, SWDAdvertisement as Advert, SWDOriginator as Orig, SWDProgram as Prog, vItem vI, Wrksta Wr WHERE Stat.AdvertisementId = Advert.AdvertisementId AND Stat.AdvertisementId = vI.Guid AND (vI.ClassGuid = "5B91F0BF-899F-49E2-B8E1-67219100BBFA" OR vI.ClassGuid="2D39BA40-2A60-42EE-92E0-C11AD2245969") AND vI.ProductGuid = "AD3F5980-D9E9-11D3-A318-0008C7A09198" AND LOWER(Prog.ProgramId) = LOWER(Advert.ProgramId) AND LOWER(Prog.CommandLine) NOT Like "aexinvsoln.exe%" AND Orig.OriginatorId = Advert.[_OriginatorId] AND Advert.[_Latest] =1 AND Orig.Type != "NSInternal" AND

37

(Stat.EventType="New Job" OR Stat.EventType="Package To Be Removed" OR Stat.EventType="Job Removed" OR Stat.EventType = "Job Updated") AND Stat. WrkstaId = Wr.WrkstaId AND (Wr.SystemType = "Win32" OR Wr.SystemType = "Win64")',N'@ProductGuid   uniqueidentifier',@ProductGuid='AD3F5980-D9E9-11D3-A318-0008C7A09198'

It is counting unique workstation ids. I change this to look at workstation names and disable the counting. Please keep in mind that this may cause you to generate a different number of machines as two machines may have ended up with the same name. For what I was doing this was ok.

Here is the sql statement for a list of machines.

exec sp_executesql N'SELECT Distinct Wr.Name FROM AeXEvt_AeX_SWD_Status as Stat, SWDAdvertisement as Advert, SWDOriginator as Orig, SWDProgram as Prog, vItem vI, Wrksta Wr WHERE Stat.AdvertisementId = Advert.AdvertisementId AND Stat.AdvertisementId = vI.Guid AND (vI.ClassGuid = "5B91F0BF-899F-49E2-B8E1-67219100BBFA" OR vI.ClassGuid="2D39BA40-2A60-42EE-92E0-C11AD2245969") AND vI.ProductGuid = "AD3F5980-D9E9-11D3-A318-0008C7A09198" AND LOWER(Prog.ProgramId) = LOWER(Advert.ProgramId) AND LOWER(Prog.CommandLine) NOT Like "aexinvsoln.exe%" AND Orig.OriginatorId = Advert.[_OriginatorId] AND Advert.[_Latest] =1 AND Orig.Type != "NSInternal" AND (Stat.EventType="New Job" OR Stat.EventType="Package To Be Removed" OR Stat.EventType="Job Removed" OR Stat.EventType = "Job Updated") AND Stat. WrkstaId = Wr.WrkstaId AND (Wr.SystemType = "Win32" OR Wr.SystemType = "Win64")',N'@ProductGuid   uniqueidentifier',@ProductGuid='AD3F5980-D9E9-11D3-A318-0008C7A09198'

Finnaly if you would like to list out all of the fields that are pulled use the following statement.

exec sp_executesql N'SELECT * FROM AeXEvt_AeX_SWD_Status as Stat, SWDAdvertisement as Advert, SWDOriginator as Orig, SWDProgram as Prog, vItem vI, Wrksta Wr WHERE Stat.AdvertisementId = Advert.AdvertisementId AND Stat. AdvertisementId = vI.Guid AND (vI.ClassGuid = "5B91F0BF-899F-49E2-B8E1-67219100BBFA" OR vI.ClassGuid="2D39BA40-2A60-42EE-92E0-C11AD2245969") AND vI.ProductGuid = "AD3F5980-D9E9-11D3-A318-0008C7A09198" AND LOWER(Prog.ProgramId) = LOWER(Advert.ProgramId) AND LOWER(Prog.CommandLine) NOT Like "aexinvsoln.exe%" AND Orig.OriginatorId = Advert.[_OriginatorId] AND Advert.[_Latest] =1 AND Orig.Type != "NSInternal" AND (Stat.EventType="New Job" OR Stat.EventType="Package To Be Removed" OR Stat.EventType="Job Removed"

```
OR Stat.EventType = "Job Updated") AND Stat.WrkstaId = Wr.WrkstaId AND
(Wr.SystemType = "Win32" OR Wr.SystemType = "Win64")',N'@ProductGuid
uniqueidentifier',@ProductGuid='AD3F5980-D9E9-11D3-
A318-0008C7A09198'
```

Now I'm off to clean up my Altiris SWD.

Posting code in wordpress

If you have ever wanted to post some source code or a code snippet in WordPress this is a sure read. Earlier today I posted an article that I wanted to post some SQL statements in. These statements were complex with lots of single and double quotes. WordPress did an excellent job of screwing these up for me. The code snippet would not work when my readers copied it and tried it themselves. Luckily I caught this before 1000's of my (nonexistent) readers could have seen it.

If WordPress has caused you some grief with formatting your code, I'm sure you have searched high and low on the internet for a plugin or even a new editor that would not mess up your text formatting. I searched the web for a few minutes myself and didn't really find what I wanted. I did come across quite a few sites that mentioned putting your quotes and double quotes as well as other characters in ASCII codes format. This seemed to be difficult for me to read through many lines of code and replace each little character that was going to possibly cause me a problem.

Replacing key characters with ASCII code keeps WordPress for formatting the text. On the output side the text is displayed correctly and is not displayed in ASCII code. The only problem I found with this solution was I had to manually figure out what to replace as well as look up the ASCII code and then type it in. My solution? A text to ASCII converter. Within seconds I found a website that would take my source code text and output ASCII codes. I simply take my entire section of source code, not just the characters that cause me problems, and I convert it to ASCII codes. I paste this into my post as if it were my code snippet (it technic-ally is, just in ASCII code format). I then use code brackets around it in my WordPress WYSIWYG editor and everything looks great.

Here is the website I used: Text to ASCII Converter Site

Hope this helps you as it has helped me.

CHAPTER 2: 2009, IT CONTINUES

New Hosting!!

Well folks I have finally purchased some real hosting. This site had been running from my home on a ubuntu server for quite some time. Before that we were hosted on a very nice dedicated server provided by a friend for free. We are now hosting on some shared hosting out of Dallas, TX. I look forward to the increased performance and bandwidth available. This should allow me to take this site to the next level.

Many things have been changing in my life and they have kept me from being able to create content on this site for some time. Hopefully this is changing. I have been promoted at work to Manager of Systems Engineering and have a team of two systems administrators working for me.

Consultants - The Good, The Bad, and the Unprofessional

Consultants are very much a part of Information Technology. There are consultants available for every part of your technology or information systems. These individuals range in skill from true experts with no one single person more skilled in their trade. While towards the bottom we get to people who really are just milking ignorance. A certain amount of honor is needed in the consulting world, mostly on the consultant's part. Usually I see consultants who are average, by this I mean they have roughly the same skill in their area as their peers do. This is usually confirmed by my peers and sometimes even the consultant themselves.

Consultants do not need always to be smarter or more of an expert in their field compared to the customers own resources. Often enough they only need to be a second set of eyes, or maybe a third party with an opinion, or even just have an impartial opinion. Having a consultant give an opinion can be beneficial for the customer only when the consultant is honest. If a consultant gives an opinion based on the idea they will benefit from it, it is worthless. It is also worthless if it is an uneducated opinion. Now I said they do not need to be experts, and this is true, however they need not lie to "sound like an expert". Giving false information is bad for the business who hired the consultant. My philosophy is if you do not know then let the customer know you are not sure but will find the correct answer. It's very unprofessional to ramble off an answer to move past the question or worse yet, blame it on someone else or some other technology.

Far too often it seems people in information technology forget that we are constantly learning. That is what makes technology great, it is always changing. You cannot be expected to know everything. You are expected to learn. A value you should have in addition to the ambition to learn is honesty. A consultant who abuses the fact that the customer is learning and then directs the customer on an incorrect path to appear better than they are should not be a consultant.

As a customer you must be on the lookout for these frauds. Information given to you by a consultant can usually be confirmed using the internet. I'm not suggesting you check everything word for word. However, if you question anything a consultant tells you, you owe it to yourself and your company to learn the correct answer.

Good consultants are an excellent resource to many business

units. I use consultants all the time. However, I ask for my consultants by name and the unprofessional ones do not come out to my location again. As we all continue to learn, it is important to remain professional.

New life for old Blackberries!

If your company is anything like mine, just about everyone has a handheld. I'll spare you the sales pitch on Blackberry, but if this is your standard handheld read on!

Blackberry's at my company are everywhere. We are liberal when it comes to giving Blackberry replacements. No real testing or troubleshooting occurs to solve the problem. We simply buy a new one and replace your old one. This has led to quite a few handhelds that allegedly have problems. Some cut out in the middle of calls or won't make calls at all. Some have been labeled as always having missed calls. Some got wet, some got scratched. Many of these devices are simply old. With no official upgrade policy in place for the software many are running old Blackberry OS's.

Recently I did some testing with a Blackberry curve. This ATT Blackberry 8310 was in decent shape but had been labeled as cutting out during calls. I took this phone home for a few days and sure enough it cuts out in the middle of calls. In this instance the user was correct to complain. These calls dropping during conversation was very annoying. A check of the Blackberry OS showed that it was running a version that was about 2 years old. A quick download later I had the latest Blackberry OS. I loaded the device manager and app loader software on my laptop and updated the 8310. Once finished the device powered on and I quickly began testing.

Much to my amazement this old curve had been granted a new life! No more dropped calls. A simple OS upgrade has fixed this phones problem. The user no doubt got a brand new $400 Blackberry by reporting this issue. Money that could have been saved with a 10-minute phone OS upgrade.

We have a box with about 150 Blackberry's in it. Various models from 8700's to 8800's. Users now are getting 9000's and 9530's. However, if we could began saving by breathing new life into our 8300's and 8800's we could save quite a few dollars. If you figure that half of the Blackberry's in our graveyard box could be restored to full health, we could save $30,000 on replacing them. Thirty thousand dollars!!! At ten minutes an upgrade it would take twenty-five hours to do all 150 devices one at a time. That's $1200 an hour you could possibly save. Who wouldn't be able to justify an employee performing these upgrades?

So, the next time you have a Blackberry come back to your IT department as broken for some reason. See if a code upgrade helps. It's faster than waiting for a new phone and quite a bit cheaper!

Thin Provision VMWare ESX Guest OS Disk

Provision your VM as normal however use a 1GB disk.
Log into your VMWare server command line via ssh or other CLI and go to the directory that contains the vmdk's for the VM.

Assuming the VM name is SERVER01 issue the following commands. If the name were different simply replace SERVER01 with your server name.
vmkfstools -i SERVER01.vmdk 1.vmdk -d thin
rm -f SERVER01*.vmdk
vmkfstools -E 1.vmdk SERVER01.vmdk

This will clone the vmdk to a new vmdk but as type thin. Then it will remove the old vmdk's. Then it will export the thin vmdk to be in place of your old one so you do not have to reconfigure the vmx.

Now log into virtual center and edit the settings for your virtual machine. Set the disk size to the maximum you wish it to be. The vmdk will appear to grow in command line. However, if you look at the vmdk in the data store it remains 1G. The space is not actually used on the vmfs volume until needed by the VM.

Blackberry Storm or Bold?

So, we've field tested both the Storm and Bold in our IT department. As a matter fact, I'm posting this very topic from outside a grocery store on my Bold. We've had at least 4 Storms issued out and a few Bolds for a several weeks for test drives. The Winner? Bold – hands down. Storm is slower both on the local system itself and Verizon's data network is notably slower than AT&T's 3G network (at least in Tulsa and Houston anyway). The only noted downside to Bold from my perspective is the battery life gives you no mercy for forgetting to charge overnight, but I'm holding out for a Gen 2 battery sometime soon. Other than that, its local operations are way fast, 3G rocks and the display is sweet too. The storm just didn't cut it for what Corporate America expects from a business PDA. In the end, it seems Bold weathered the Storm.

Citrix and High-Demand Graphics (pwned)

If you're familiar with Citrix from an administrative perspective, then publishing apps to the outside world is nothing new to you. Whether it's for a Systems Administrator at EMCWorld in Las Vegas ◆◆ or a C-level executive on holiday in Italy, Citrix Metaframe is a widely-used tool (and for good reason). If you're a larger shop with multiple sites, you're likely familiar with publishing in-house applications across a WAN as well. And finally, if you work for a company like mine, you may have been (lucky to be) in a situation where everyone in the science department just HAD to have double 30-inch monitors with graphics cards hot enough to handle *Crysis*, and now their Citrix application has graphics issues. Undoubtedly, the ticket will come in entitled "Citrix not working – Please fix" with "ASAP" urgency or something to this effect. The problem? Well, the problem isn't their (2400 x OMG!) resolution, because that's completely understandable based on what your users are up to, right? Maybe. The real problem is that if the high-res application they want to run happens to be a published

Citrix application on a CPS 4.0 system, you may have maxed the ceiling on your graphics memory allocation for ICA sessions.

This was a headache for a little while for me, but there's nothing quite like a good "w00t!" moment when you finally nail a solution. We had visited and revisited the graphics settings for the published app itself, and for the farm from the management console, but nothing seemed to quite hit the spot until a bit of research turned up a little golden nugget. What did it for us was finding a registry tweak that increases the farm-level default maximum graphics buffer setting from 8MB (supported by Citrix) to up to 16MB as an actual max (not so supported by Citrix). This default setting can be found in the Metaframe Management Console under Farm properties and ICA settings, but hold your horses there, cowboy! The management console will never allow you to set more than 8MB as the max, but if you apply the tweak shared below, you might be able to return to your... err, ahem... "Internet traffic filtering test environment" sooner than later.

Before I finish up, I'd like to make a side note. Citrix is supposed to have addressed graphics issues in CPS 4.5, or "XenApp" if you prefer, in relation to high-end graphics demands, but I haven't had an opportunity yet to test those waters. XenApp uses what Citrix calls SpeedScreen Progressive Display (allegedly better than regular SpeedScreen). Citrix specifically gives a nod to medical imaging and GIS mapping applications with this technology, so it sounds like they are looking at the right apps for high-end graphics requirements. It also boasts support for multiple monitors. If anyone running 4.5 can attest, please leave us a note here about it. Perhaps Citrix deserves an "atta boy", but only time will tell.

At any rate, there were a few versions of this fix out there, but most of them were based partly on fact and partly on assumption (or they were just plain lazy). Only one version I found was based on viable science and math. Don't be afraid to use math in your solutions... it will only make you a more accurate admin. Not everyone can throw a bunch numbers together like my SE, and then spit them out in 3 seconds flat. The solution for that is called calc.exe. ☺

This is the solution I documented for my company:

Registry key: HKLM\SYSTEM\CurrentControlSet\Control\Terminal Server\Wds\icawd\thin16

MaxLVBMem registry setting: There is no one setting that is perfect for everyone. A little 5th grade math is required to find the right entry for this registry tweak, but it's easy. You'll need three things: Desired user screen resolution height and width (i.e. 1024×768 or whatever). We'll call them "h" and "w". And then you'll need the color bit depth in use which we'll call "d". The bit depth max for Citrix is 24 bit. Here's the equation you should use: $(h \times w \times d)/8 = v$ [where v = the registry value needed]. This will give you a unique number for your environment in bytes. So if a user has a 1024×768 resolution (with Citrix's 24 bit color depth max), it would look like so:

(1024 x 768 x 24)/8 = 2359296. In this case, 2359296 would be the decimal value in bytes you want to use for your decimal value in this registry setting. Keep in mind, nothing over 16MB will matter.

This only needs to be applied to the server(s) on which the applications requiring advanced graphics are published. Because more resources are being allocated toward graphics, this will be a performance hit. How much of a hit depends on how many users who have high-end video cards will be hitting up your Citrix server(s) for major graphics. Load balancing may become crucial at this point if you're not doing it already.

Important note: The Farm will successfully reset this registry key any time farm settings are edited in the future, so permissions must be set to **deny the System account the "set value" rights** on this registry key.

Enjoy – mn

Virtual Machine File System - VMFS

Virtual Machine File System – VMFS

I was asked a question today and I thought it might be a good idea to begin posting the answers to some of the questions I am asked.

What is VMFS?

VMFS is Virtual Machine File System. It's just the file system that exists on the VMWare ESX servers.
In it exists files one of which is vmdk, virtual machine disk.
The is the VM guest itself. Instead of the virtual machines having a hard drive they have a vmdk.
All the vmdk's are contained on a vmfs. Vmfs, ntfs, fat, fat32 these are all file systems.

Media Keyboard - Open Winamp

Here is a tip for you music listeners. Have you ever wanted to have your media key on your cheap dell keyboard to open Winamp by default instead of windows media player? If so you can accomplish this by setting Winamp to be the default player for CD's.

Central Knowledge Repository -- vMedic

Well the day has finally come for us. This site has had such great success that we have been acquired for **1.3 billion** dollars by a company created between VMWare, Microsoft, EMC, Dell, Intel, and Cisco. The sub company known as **vMedic** has been created to oversee and maintain a centralized knowledge repository for the major parent companies. vMedic will likely save the lives of millions of Systems Engineers.

All existing knowledge base articles, documentation, white papers and other technical information will be rewritten into thesystemsengineer.com formats. This will allow for fast response to today's issues without the need to discover, remember, or creatively come up with search patterns that may or may not get the intended results. The original owner of The Systems Engineer will continue to take an active role in keeping the flow of information hot and up to date. Although major funding is being provided through the channels between the parent company's and the sub company vMedic, advertisements will still be needed to stay afloat.

New authors and editors will be found to assist with new content creation. The backing of vMedic will allow for furious growth. We are all very excited here about this announcement. As soon as the announcements are up on the parent sites we will link to them.

For now, please continue to make us the best site for information on today's Systems Engineering needs.

Thank you!
vMedic – Saving SE's one at a time.

April Fools.

TSM 6.1 Client - 5.5 ODBC

If you are using the new 6.1 client, you can use the 5.5 odbc driver. Tested and working on vista x64.

Cisco Live

I will be headed out to San Francisco Sunday for Cisco Live 2009. Hope to find some new solutions to some challenges we face. Some items of interest to me are RFID, B2B Telepresence, Business Video, Nexus, and VOIP monitoring.

If anyone wants to meet up for discussion on various topics let me know. I'd be happy to share my experience in the field.

See you there!

ESX to EMC Clariion Lun Map

An easy way to find WWNN of a Clariion LUN inside of ESX.

esxcfg-mpath -lv | grep ^Disk | grep -v vmhba0 | awk '{print $3,$5,$2}' | cut -b15-

Outlook 2007 Logon Prompt on Exchange

When using Outlook 2007 with Exchange 2007 some of our users would get prompted to login to the client access server. Clicking cancel would still allow them in their mailbox with what appeared to be all functionality. However, the prompt would return after a few minutes. This was very annoying as you can imagine. After some web searching I was able to find the problem along with a solution.

First open up Exchange 2007 powershell. We'll check on the problem and verify it is the same as well as fix it from here.

Run the following command.

[PS] C:\Windows\System32>Get-ClientAccessServer | fl

Name : EXCH03

OutlookAnywhereEnabled : False

AutoDiscoverServiceCN : exch03

AutoDiscoverServiceClassName : ms-Exchange-AutoDiscover-Service
AutoDiscoverServiceInternalUri : https://exch03.company.com/Autodiscover/
Autodiscover.xml

AutoDiscoverServiceGuid : 77378f46-2c66-4aa9-a6a6-3e7a48b19596

AutoDiscoverSiteScope : {DownTown}

IsValid : True

OriginatingServer : ADDC01.company.com

ExchangeVersion : 0.1 (8.0.535.0)
DistinguishedName : CN=EXCH03,CN=Servers,CN=Exchange Administrative
Group (FYDIBOHF23SPDLT),CN=Administ
rative Groups,CN=PHE,CN=Microsoft Exchange,CN=Services,CN=Configur-
ation,DC=company,D

C=com

Identity : EXCH03

Guid : 341169c4-dd14-47b2-b3e6-01ca8653dfbb
ObjectCategory : company.com/Configuration/Schema/ms-Exch-Exchange-
Server

ObjectClass : {top, server, msExchExchangeServer}

WhenChanged : 4/22/2009 10:03:06 AM

WhenCreated : 4/7/2009 10:37:52 AM

Name : EXCH04

OutlookAnywhereEnabled : False

AutoDiscoverServiceCN : EXCH04

AutoDiscoverServiceClassName : ms-Exchange-AutoDiscover-Service
AutoDiscoverServiceInternalUri : https://mail.company.com/autodiscover/
autodiscover.xml

AutoDiscoverServiceGuid : 77378f46-2c66-4aa9-a6a6-3e7a48b19596

AutoDiscoverSiteScope : {DownTown}

```
IsValid : True
OriginatingServer : ADDC01.company.com
ExchangeVersion : 0.1 (8.0.535.0)
DistinguishedName  :  CN=EXCH04,CN=Servers,CN=Exchange Administrative
Group (FYDIBOHF23SPDLT),CN=Administ
rative   Groups,CN=PHE,CN=Microsoft   Exchange,CN=Services,CN=Configur-
ation,DC=company,D
C=com
Identity : EXCH04
Guid : 4857fd2e-da32-4a7c-a97a-cfb0135d2875
ObjectCategory   :   company.com/Configuration/Schema/ms-Exch-Exchange-
Server
ObjectClass : {top, server, msExchExchangeServer}
WhenChanged : 4/13/2009 12:46:00 PM
WhenCreated : 4/13/2009 10:07:00 AM
```

You should notice here that our AutoDiscoverServiceInternalUri points to our external dns name for Outlook Web Access. This is our problem. This should be the internal dns name for our client access server. Here is the command to set it to what we want.

```
[PS] C:\Windows\System32>Set-ClientAccessServer -Identity "EXCH04" -Auto-
discoverServiceInternalURI "https://exch04
.company.com/Autodiscover/Autodiscover.xml"
[PS] C:\Windows\System32>
```

VMWorld 2009 - San Francisco

Well I am here in San Francisco for VMWorld 2009. If I find any good content, I'll be sure to post it here. If anyone would like to meet up for conversation, white boarding, or to share war stories you can email me.

VMworld 2009 - San Francisco - Labs

VMworld organizers,

I hope you take the suggestions of the attendees. More labs were needed. The vsphere performance lab was slap full each time I tried to get in. Many of us were turned away. Then we attempted to get into other labs and they were each full or past the start time and the conference workers would not let additional people in. The only other activity available at the time was the self-paced labs. The line for the self-paced labs had about 400 people in it.

More content is required to keep us busy on Monday's. I eventually did make it into two labs but wish to attend more. We will just skip talking about the no lunch on Monday issue.

/rant

VMworld 2009 - CiRBA grid match

Well folks it is time for the 2nd annual CiRBA grid match at VMworld!

This year they have taken notice to our methods of winning and have added a twitter draw to their ways to win.

Here is a list of what you can win.
1. Twitter Draw $250 Best Buy gift card. September 4th, 2009.
2. Daily Draw $500 Best Buy gift card. September 1-3, 2009.
3. Grand Prize $1000 Best Buy gift card. September 3, 2009.

So, everyone takes a picture, so we can match up these grids.

Here is mine.

VMworld - SRM Developers

Last night I spent two hours talking to a couple of developers from the Site Recovery Manager group. They turned out to be excellent people who listened to my experiences with SRM. I felt empowered as a small voice for the SRM user base. They were already aware of some of the issues I addressed, others seemed to spark their interest.

IP customization obviously needs work. An enterprise class user interface is needed, and it should not look like a spreadsheet. We talked about policy and rule-based IP customization. This would work well in my environment since I change the 2nd and 3rd octet. For example, in site A you may have the IP address 10.20.30.40. In site B this machine would have its IP changed to 10.40.130.40. The 10.40.30.0/24 network is already in use as a server VLAN (VLAN 30) there. Policy or rule based, in the inventory mappings possibly, would let me say that I want the destination IP to always have 100 added to the 3rd octet and use 40 for the 2nd octet if the 2nd octet is 20. Then I would never have to do anything else for IP's. Of course, exceptions and additional expressions would be awesome.

Failback is another key point. Currently SRM is a one-way product. You set it all up, test your plan to prove success, and you wait for an event that justifies hitting that red run button. Now you are up and running in a new and strange place, but with no easy way back. You must create your IP customizations and build your protection group and recovery plans. The ability to do all of this ahead of time needs to be there. Your protection group should have a failover and a failback plan section of the recovery plan. Your configurations should be stored in both sites. It would be nice to be able to test the failback as well, however this could get complicated I would think.

Deep recovery plan testing is something you can do now, but it requires considerable development on the customer end. Of course, I am talking about proving your recovery plan beyond simply having the virtual machine power up. A virtual machine is useless! It's what we have running in them that matters most. Exchange, Citrix, DNS, Active Directory, Oracle, or SQL insert any number of applications and services you may use, these are what you are after. You can write your own scripts to check that these functions. Then have exit codes from the scripts that let SRM say if a VM had an error and thus the DR plan. It would be excellent if VMWare provided these scripts for the default installations of major applications like Exchange or SQL. In addition, a place for the VMWare user community to post their own scripts. I would really like to see more than just checking for a process to be running but will take anything. This would also lead us into scheduling DR tests in the middle of the night or weekend. We can sleep while the systems make sure the DR plan is good once a week. Notify of results with an email you check on Monday. I think this is the future of DR tests. If VMWare doesn't do it someone else will.

Test bubbles are also something I would like to see improved. Currently the test bubble is there just to allow testing to work on a single ESX host. You can create an isolated VLAN (OSI layer 2) to allow VM's to communicate across ESX hosts. However, there is no built-in solution to allow for routing. We have tackled this at my shop with a Linux machine running in the recovery site as a VM. It has 4 virtual nics and I have created 3 isolated vlans for testing my servers. The fourth virtual nic is available if needed to allow internet connectivity to the machines for testing. This allows me to have a 3-subnet test bubble with routing inside of it. VMWare could package up a quick appliance with a web interface that you could configure all the subnets and it would create virtual nics for you. There are obvious issues that could come up if you allow your test machines to communicate with production or the internet. An example would be an email server brought up in test allowed to connect to internet and delivering email even the its production twin already did.

I would like to give a big THANK YOU to the developers standing at the SRM station in the VMWare booth. It was a pleasure speaking to you. I really do appreciate your work on SRM. The product is wonderful and appears to have an excellent future.

Shared hosting security issues?

I was helping a friend with his shared hosting account and found an interesting security issue. Gallery is a popular open source and free photo management system. I found a way for you to escape a jailed or chroot account using gallery on this host.

This shared hosting account made / your /home/username directory. Username was the username used to log into to their hosting software cPanel. Using gallery, you can go to the import section of site-admin. Then click web/server. Here we add / as the directory to look in. Now we can go to an album and choose to add item. Click the tab at the top for local file system. Next, we simply hit find files and now we can browse / on the server. We can go to /home and see all the other user accounts on this server.

I was able to browse some of the other user directories while working with the hosting providers support to show them the issue. I was even able to add pictures to my gallery from another user's home directory. By having the usernames listed in home we have half of the two-part authentication, username and password. I reported this issue to the hosting provider and they are looking into it.

To protect yourself make sure you backup your information on your shared hosting. Also, please keep your password secure and make sure it doesn't contain any part of your username. Next you should make sure your file permissions are set correctly in your home directory. Finally follow your hosting providers security best practices.

After some additional testing since I started writing this I have discovered a few more pieces of information. I uploaded phpsh which allowed me to execute commands from a php site. I quickly ran whoami as I was thinking apache may have been running as apache or root. Turns out it is only running as my username for my session. However, it is apparently not running jailed. Although I could see /root/ I was unable to access it.

A New Data Center

Well I am building a new data center and have some interesting things to research. Some new trends have emerged since the last time I had to participate in anything like this. Some of them make great sense and others seem like the same old way with a new spin.

One new item that has caught my interest is to run the equipment on higher voltage such as 208 single phases. This allows for some power efficiencies as well as allows for some bigger power strips. Along with this goes metered power distribution units. Some vendors have these available in 24 c13 plugs which is nice since I am running 4 pdu's to a rack right now. Going down to just two will be a bit neater.

Another trend is hot isle containment. A few vendors have different ways of doing this currently. One vendor builds a box out of your racks by putting doors and a roof on a group of them to form a pod. Another vendor puts chimneys on the back of your racks and sends heat to the plenum in the ceiling. If you have a raised floor with underfloor cooling this second method seems great. If you have spot cooling or in row cooling the first method seems to be a better fit. I have read some articles that say cold isle containment is better however it has a downfall. People who enter the data center will always be warm or hot. I like a cold data center myself.

The last trend that has caught my interest is physical security and monitoring. The prices on equipment and software to accomplish this has come down quite a bit.

I'm interested in comments around this topic if you have them.

Reset Symantec Altiris Helpdesk Solution incident numbers

Plenty of times I have reset my helpdesk incident number to 1 when implementing or testing. To do this you need to make sure all the incidents have been deleted. Next in SQL Management Studio you need to open the Altiris_Incidents database and edit the workitem_next_number table. Change the value of next_number to one number before what you want the next incident to be. If you want to reset to 1 then this number needs to be zero.

If you had a slew of incidents created on accident from an auto reply to your helpdesk then you may need to change it to maybe 12860. 12860 is your current last incident and the next new incident will be 12860.

I have used this many times and have had no real issues that I can find.

Enjoy!

CHAPTER 3: 2010, THE YEAR OF FIREFIGHTING AND HISTORY.

See who is using Symantec Altiris Helpdesk Solution licenses

Here is a quick SQL query that will display who is using your Symantec Altiris Helpdesk Solution licenses.

```
exec sp_executesql N'select * from HD_worker_view where worker_active_access = "1"',N'@ProductGuid uniqueidentifier',@ProductGuid='FCA7F0B7-B61B-4979-946E-C921B85F2A39'
```

Enjoy

Topeka - Google? April Fools!

A different kind of company name

Early last month the mayor of Topeka, Kansas stunned the world by announcing that his city was changing its name to Google. We've been wondering ever since how best to honor that moving gesture. Today we are pleased to announce that as of 1 AM (Central Daylight Time) April 1st, Google has officially changed our name to Topeka.

We didn't reach this decision lightly; after all, we had a fair amount of brand equity tied up in our old name. But the more we surfed around (the former) Topeka's municipal website, the more kinship we felt with this fine city at the edge of the Great Plains.

In fact, Topeka Google Mayor Bill Bunten expressed it best: "Don't be fooled. Even Google recognizes that all roads lead to Kansas, not just yellow brick ones."

For 150 years, its fortuitous location at the confluence of the Kansas River and the Oregon Trail has made the city formerly known as Topeka a key jumping-off point to the new world of the West, just as for 150 months the company formerly known as Google has been a key jumping-off point to the new world of the web. When in 1858 a crucial bridge built across the Kansas River was destroyed by flooding mere months later, it was promptly rebuilt — and we too are accustomed to releasing 2.0 versions of software after stormy feedback on our 'beta' releases. And just as the town's nickname is "Top City," and the word "topeka" itself derives from a term used by the Kansa and Ioway tribes to refer to "a good place to dig for potatoes," we'd like to think that our website is one of the web's top places to dig for information.

In the early 20th century, the former Topeka enjoyed a remarkable run of political prominence, gracing the nation with Margaret Hill McCarter, the first woman to address a national political convention (1920, Republican); Charles Curtis, the only Native American ever to serve as vice president ('29 to '33, under Herbert Hoover); Carrie Nation, leader of the old temperance movement (and wielder of American history's most famous hatchet); and, most important, Alfred E. Neuman, arguably the most influential figure to an entire generation of Americans. We couldn't be happier to add our own chapter to this storied history.

A change this dramatic won't happen without consequences, perhaps even some disruptions. Here are a few of the thorny issues that we hope everyone in the broader Topeka community will bear in mind as we begin one of the most important transitions in our company's history:

•Correspondence to both our corporate headquarters and offices around the world should now be addressed to Topeka Inc., but otherwise can be addressed normally.

•Google employees once known as "Googlers" should now be referred to as either "Topekers" or "Topekans," depending on the result of a board meeting that's ongoing at this hour. Whatever the outcome, the conclusion is clear: we aren't in Google anymore.

•Our new product names will take some getting used to. For instance, we'll have to assure users of Topeka News and Topeka Maps that these services will continue to offer news and local information from across the globe. Topeka Talk, similarly, is an instant messaging product, not, say, a folksy midwestern morning show. And Project Virgle, our co-venture with Richard Branson and Virgin to launch the first permanent human colony on Mars, will henceforth be known as Project Vireka.

•We don't really know what to tell Oliver Google Kai's parents, except that, if you ask us, Oliver Topeka Kai would be a charming name for their little boy.

•As our lawyers remind us, branded product names can achieve such popularity as to risk losing their trademark status (see cellophane, zippers, trampolines, et al). So, we hope all of you will do your best to remember our new name's proper usage:

Firefly. Bring this show back please

I loved this show. Why did they have to cancel it? I recently watched the season again and remained as entertained as ever. I rented the movie based on it called Serenity. I have seen it a few times and it is still good.

Firefly was a space western. A space western! What an awesome concept, one that has even influenced shows such as Star Trek and

Star Wars. In Firefly a crew on board of a space ship struggle to survive in a post war universe. I highly suggest checking it out.

Cisco Unified Computing Solution - First Thoughts

I have been working on implementing this solution from Cisco. At first, I was a little skeptical that Cisco made a good choice entering the server world. Cisco has done an excellent job in the network world. This appears to have carried over to the server world.

I'm curiously considering referring to Cisco as a data center company not a networking company.

I really do like the VCE combination. I've been running VMware and EMC in my data center for 5 years. After spending many weeks researching Cisco UCS and their competition I'm happy to add Cisco to the mix. So far everything they have designed into the solution makes perfect sense. The palo adapter has been the solution to many problems I have white boarded. The further I get into UCS the more I like it.

Clariion F.A.S.T. V1 costs money?

EMC has a long track record of providing excellent tools to manage their products. Navicli is an example of a product that is included with your Clariion. EMC maintains up to date versions for any platform you can imagine, aix, linux, hpux, windows, vmware, etc. This tool allows you to perform many commands on your Clariion platform. EMC released some new technology called F.A.S.T which stands for Fully Automated Storage Tiering. This is really a bundle of 3 tools and is called F.A.S.T. V1.

The 3 tools are Navi Analyzer, Navisphere QoS, and Fast LUN Migrator. Let's think about this for a bit. Everyone should already have Navi Analyzer. I always purchase it for my arrays. I also already own QoS. Now I am forced to buy them again to get the new tool Fast LUN Migrator. The reason for this? FLM requires .nar files to work! It cannot function with .naz files which you can always generate without Navi Analyzer. Rather than release the ability for you to analyzer .naz files with their tool and restrict you from opening them with an analyzer interface they force you to buy navi analyzer. I have yet to see why you need QoS as it is not used by Analyzer or FLM. It appears this is just an extra. The price for the suite you ask? You could buy a giant nexus one phone instead.

The installation of FLM is only 64MB, almost 1$ per byte. None of this is adding up to value for me yet. Let's look at what FLM does for us. We already know what Analyzer and QoS brings to the table, the mystery is this new tool that we must pay so much for.

FLM is a command line tool for windows. Here is how it works.
1. You download a nar file from your array.
2. You run fastlunmigrator.exe lunanalyze narfile.nar
3. You open a csv file and type in destination raid groups for the luns that are recommended to move.
4. You run fastlunmigrator.exe lunassist -h ipaddr -user adminuser -password adminpass -scope 0 -file narfileout.csv
5. You wait for the LUN to migrate to the destination raid group. You can check status with fastlunmigrator.exe -status -h ipaddr -user adminuser -password adminpass -scope 0
6. Once it says complete for step 5 above, you are done.

Now what happened in step 1? Well you used analyzer to get the nar file if you did not own analyzer you would get a naz file. In step 2 the FLM product looked for luns with over 70% utilization or an average busy queue length of greater than 5 or a response time over 30 ms. If it finds one, then it reports in the csv that it needs to move to faster disk type. In step 3 you MANUALLY choose raid groups and type them into the csv so that FLM knows where to move the source LUN to. In step 4 FLM is creating a new LUN of the proper size in the destination raid group, this is the destination LUN. It then does a LUN migration to this LUN from the source LUN. Step 5 is just a textual report of migration summary.

Now all of this can simply be scripted. Many shops may already even have this scripted. This Fast LUN Migrator tool should be free. The real power is analyzer. It is the one that is providing all of the data. Everything else can be done in Clariion manually. In fact, you would likely do LUN migrations one at a time anyways. Could you imagine if NaviCLI was a paid for product?

Now EMC has announced that F.A.S.T. v2 is coming out. This is sub LUN tiering and sounds very interesting. There are some articles on the internet that mention EMC may be behind the curve here since some of their competition already have very similar features. F.A.S.T v2 and Flash Cache will be two emerging paid for features for Clariion to keep an eye on. Oh did I mention F.A.S.T. v2 is not an upgrade to F.A.S.T. in the sense you get it with your maintenance. No, F.A.S.T. v2 is a PAID for in addition to F.A.S.T. v1. They are going to hit you twice, that's right folks.

EMC,
You have made a mistake here in charging for Fast LUN Migrator. This product should be free. I wasn't overly surprised you charged for it at first because I thought it did more. At first, I thought it would be sub $10,000. To find it is almost 6 times that list price is shocking. I keep looking for what you think is worth so much and I do plan to investigate more. Charge for F.A.S.T. v2 not v1.

EMC World 2010 - The journey to the private cloud

EMC World 2010 is coming to an end. I am in my last session here and finally have some time to update you all on what I have seen. Really it is what everyone has seen as it was announced here. The star of the show, VPlex. This allows for active/active storage using synchronous distances.

The theme this year is "The Journey to the Private Cloud". My company started this journey years ago so it's nice to get a conference dedicated to what we have been working to accomplish for years. We have been looking for some technology to allow us to "flip the switch". We want our workloads to be mobile and unbolted from the physical machines. This process started with VMware many years ago. As we close in on 95% of the workloads virtualized the next task is to unbolt the workload from the data center.

Now moving a workload from a data center has been possible for a while. However, moving that workload back has been tricky. The main factor is time and effort. You could restore a work load and then update clients to point towards it. Then you had to do the same to go back. VMware SRM made this a little easier, but it isn't quite "flip the switch".

Flipping the switch is an action. We want this to be a repeatable action. We want the effort to reduce to a minimum as well as the time. Days and Weeks is not good enough for us to be able to move a workload. Hours is better but still not what we are looking for. We want minutes and seconds. We also do not want the workload to be halted when we "flip the switch". This meant a few things had to exist that just were not possible until recently. You needed uninterrupted network access to the workload. You also needed writable access to the data in all locations. You then need the workload to move between physical computing devices without interruption.

Moving a workload between physical computing devices is possible with vMotion when using VMware. This has been in existence for many years but only inside of a data center.

Cisco has solved the issue of uninterrupted network access to the workload with Nexus. A new paid for feature for Nexus 7K's called Overlay Transport Virtualization. OTV allows for stretching a VLAN but stops all the bad stuff your network people will tell you about doing this. The IP of the VM now does not have to change even though it is running in a data center that is 100km away from where it was.

EMC has solved the uninterrupted access to storage, both reading and writing. Active/Active access to storage with disks that are separated by 100km. VPlex allows for synchronous access to both storage arrays while presenting a single LUN to the vSphere host.

You then simply vMotion the VM and no one is the wiser. This is all brand-new technology and information is trickling out about it. The next year or so will be very interesting with this new capability. EMC has said they are working on increasing to asynchronous distances which will open a new world to mobile workloads.

Very interesting indeed.

Cisco X-Prize Car

Cisco's 3-wheel car. Looks awesome. Sitting in Mandalay Bar at Cisco Live Networkers 2010.

Increasing Linux Virtual Disks on VMware

Record the results of the following command
fdisk -u -l /dev/sda

Disk /dev/sda: 8589 MB, 8589934592 bytes
255 heads, 63 sectors/track, 1044 cylinders, total 16777216 sectors
Units = sectors of 1 * 512 = 512 bytes

Device Boot Start End Blocks Id System
/dev/sda1 * 63 208844 104391 83 Linux
/dev/sda2 208845 16771859 8281507+ 8e Linux LVM

Increase the VMDK (snapshot)
Reboot to see new space
fdisk /dev/sda

```
p
d
2
n
p
2
default should be beginning
t
2
8e
x
b
2
Use the number from fdisk -u -l /dev/sda you recorded. Should be
the start of sda2
w
reboot
vgdisplay
Should see note the free pe on volgroup00
pvresize /dev/sda2
vgdisplay
note the new free pe on volgroup00
swapoff -v /dev/VolGroup00/LogVol01
lvresize /dev/VolGroup00/Logvol01 -L +11G
mkswap /dev/VolGroup00/LogVol01
swapon -va
free to see new swap space
```

Firefighter

In January 2010 I saw a sign when entering my neighborhood that
was from the local fire department. The sign was asking for volun-
teers. Just like any boy growing up I had always loved firefighters.
So, I decided to check out the URL they had posted on the sign.

I found an interesting event that they put on every year for the past few years called Citizens Fire Academy. This was right up my alley. I was a citizen of Jersey Village and I had some interest in what the "firefighters" were all about. I remember thinking, who are these firefighters? What do they do when they are not fighting fires? What is fighting a fire anyway, spraying water?

Citizens fire academy lasted about 3 months, every Thursday night and two Saturdays. This turned out to be one of the most interesting things I have done in the past few years. I learned more about the fire service than I even knew existed. I was certified by the red cross in CPR and First Aid by the second class. The fire science classes were the deal sealer for me. I was fascinated. I'll admit I was quite the firebug as a kid. I made my own fireworks and firecrackers. I realized in one of the fire science classes that I still had the fascination of fire in me. What had changed was that I was getting the proper education in a safe and controlled (as much as possible, it is fire) environment. The instructor performed live fire experiments and demonstrations, that simply proved what was myth and what was fact.

About a month into the Citizens fire academy, a ~400-hour cadet class started. Joining the fire service as a volunteer and completing the training would turn me into a real firefighter, albeit a newbie. I couldn't pass up the opportunity. I started in late January, "First Responder" training with Cy-Fair. First Responder is the medical portion of training that is required by Cy-Fair. After finishing this section of the training, I felt more comfortable knowing the information. Skills like back boarding, c-spine stabilization, splinting, CPR, and recognizing common medical issues are important and were well taught. During this time, I was still attending Citizens fire academy, absorbing as much knowledge as I could.

Over the next 5 months I endured and survived some of the most fun, exciting, and difficult training I have been through. The best summary, "15 minutes of work fully packed up is equal to 2 hours of cardio". I heard a Houston firefighter say that, I won't even fact check it because I was ready to collapse after 27 minutes of work fully packed up. I got to do this during consumption test which was to find out how long we last on a 30-minute air bottle. We did so many things like ladders, hoses, live burns, ventilation, air duct mazes, ropes, tools, and SCBA to name a few.

We were quickly broken up into teams and my team was like fire family. Jim, Brendon, Eric, and I made up Team 5. We looked out for each other, checking gear, repeating instructions, you name it. This was very important because quite honestly our lives depended on it. The fire didn't care that we were just cadets.

We all survived the training and graduated in June.

Upgrading Atape device driver in AIX

It seems I am always upgrading tape formats to keep up with my growth. I have decided it would be best for the procedure I follow to be well documented. I use Atape for the drives and I use the Tivoli Storage Manager driver for the library. This is the method I follow for configuring the drives.

1) From TSM:
Save the output from the device queries, and save the current device configuration (the filename is optional):

query library
query drive f=d
query path f=d
query devclass f=d
backup devconfig [filename=devconfig.bak]

2) From AIX:
List the tape devices:

lsdev -Cc tape

Remove the drive and library device names:

rmdev -dl

For example, if the drive device name is /dev/rmt1:

rmdev -dl rmt1

3) Upgrade Atape
Ftp the Atape driver in binary mode from ftp://index.storsys.ibm.com/devdrvr/AIX or ftp://ftp.software.ibm.com/storage/devdrvr/AIX

Remove the older Atape driver (optional):

installp -u Atape.driver

Install and commit the Atape driver. For example, if you downloaded the file to /tmp/Atape.12.0.8.0.bin:

installp -acXd /tmp/Atape.12.0.8.0.bin all

Configure the tape device:

cfgmgr -v

(-v is not required but will show where it hangs if it does)

Verify the new devices are Available:

lsdev -Cc tape

(Note: While not always necessary, it is strongly recommended to reboot the system after upgrading the Atape.driver)

4) From TSM:
While it is recommended to remove and redefine the paths after any hardware change, including upgrading Atape.driver, sometimes it is not necessary to do anything else after upgrading Atape. If the activity log reports I/O errors for the library or drives, sometimes it is only necessary to force the TSM server to communicate with the drives to resolve them:

update path srctype=server desttype=drive library= device= online=yes

If this does not resolve the I/O errors, then continue with steps 5-7.

5) Delete the drive and library paths
For each drive:

delete path srctype=server desttype=drive library=

For the library:

delete path srctype=server desttype=library

6) Redefine the drive and library paths

define path srctype=server desttype=library device=/dev/ on-line=yes
define path srctype=server desttype=library library= device-name=/dev/ online=yes

(Use the devconfig file as a guide for the definitions.)

References:
IBM Tivoli Storage Manager for AIX Administrator's Reference
Atape device driver README ftp://index.storsys.ibm.com/dev-drvr/AIX/README

Change a FC drive in TSM on AIX

If you run your TSM on AIX read on...

Tape drives need to be changed out from time to time. The process can get tricky if you don't remember the steps. I'll give them to you in a bit and you can always reference this page when you need to perform this action again. This is test on AIX 5.3 and Tivoli 5.5.

Step 1. Log into TSM and determine which drive you need to change. You can use query drive, show library and query path f=d to get this information. Let's assume it is a drive named "DRIVE00" and that its path is /dev/rmt0.

Step 2. Delete the path definition in TSM for the Drive. An example command would be "del path server1 drive00 srct=server destt=drive library0. You can run a help delete path. Remember the settings because we can use them later.

Step 3. Delete the drive definition in TSM. An example command would be "del drive

rmdev -dl lb0
rmdev -dl rmt1
rmdev -dl rmt2
rmdev -dl rmt3

Smit, Devices, Tivoli, Discover Supported Devices, Both fscsi adapters. This gives us lb's and mt's. We do not want mt's.

rmdev -dl mt0
rmdev -dl mt1
rmdev -dl mt2

run cfgmgr in aix to get the rmt's back.

delete path ZPHBACKUP01 DRIVE00 SRCT=SERV DESTT=DR LIBR=ML6020
delete path ZPHBACKUP01 DRIVE01 SRCT=SERV DESTT=DR LIBR=ML6020
delete path ZPHBACKUP01 DRIVE02 SRCT=SERV DESTT=DR LIBR=ML6020
delete path ZPHBACKUP01 ML6020 SRCT=SERV DESTT=LIBR

delete drive ML6020 DRIVE00
delete drive ML6020 DRIVE01
delete drive ML6020 DRIVE02

stop/start tivoli storage manager

define path ZPHBACKUP01 ML6020 SRCT=SERV DESTT=LIBR DEVI=/dev/lb0

def drive ML6020 DRIVE00
def drive ML6020 DRIVE01
def drive ML6020 DRIVE02

```
define path ZPHBACKUP01 DRIVE00 SRCT=SERV DESTT=DRIVE
LIBR=ML6020 DEVI=/dev/rmt0
define path ZPHBACKUP01 DRIVE01 SRCT=SERV DESTT=DRIVE
LIBR=ML6020 DEVI=/dev/rmt1
define path ZPHBACKUP01 DRIVE02 SRCT=SERV DESTT=DRIVE
LIBR=ML6020 DEVI=/dev/rmt2
```

Historical Apollo 16 Audio - Thanks NASA!

I'm sitting here doing some work on VMware view listening to Historical Apollo 16 Audio recordings. These guys communicate quite well. It's amazing how professional and well these guys communicate.

John Watts Young (Johnny) and Charles Moss Duke, Jr. (Charlie) have been working on the surface of the moon for the last hour. Drilling holes, fixing air hoses, taking pictures, etc. The culture of my world is different from these guys. I'll make a conscious effort to be more like these guys in the future. Even Houston is impressive. They are blunt when they need to be, passive at the right times, and generally able to show the excitement of standing on the moon.

Hah, "sound doesn't travel too good in a vacuum, but it jumped", they are taking some pictures.

Soma.fm is an online radio station that I use sometimes. One of the streams is Mission Control audio. I'm here in my chair living this event for the first time along with some ambient chillout style music. You see, I was not even born when these guys were making history. Some 238,000 miles from earth and 9 years before I was born. I'm sure they never thought anyone would be listening to this in their homes 29 years later.

Mr. Young & Mr. Duke, I really appreciate all you have done for the space program. I hope you are both enjoying retirement. I am enjoying listening to the fine job you guys did. Would love to meet you if you are ever in Houston.

Intel to buy McAfee

I did not see this one coming. I do see some reasons for it and some benefits, just didn't expect to see it.

McAfee makes some nice products for the enterprise. ePolicy Orchestrator is something I really like, use daily, and have used for almost ten years. McAfee Virus Scan Enterprise 7.0+ has been leaps and bounds better than 4.5. 8.7i is wonderful. Some of the features I use are custom file access denial rules to block read and write to PST files. This allowed for PST to be completely eradicated in my shop and for us to meet our email policies. ePolicy's rogue system detection is another amazing piece.

I suppose processor based anti-malware could be interesting. Time will tell. You have my attention Intel. McAfee already has my business.

VMworld 2010 First Impressions

VMworld 2010 so far has been informative. It's obvious in my first few sessions that VMware is serious about cloud computing. Most of my sessions have either shown or eluded to upcoming cloud-oriented products and tools from VMware. They appear to even be providing the software we will need to really run our own private clouds. This appears to heavily depend on orchestrator. Keep an eye out for vCloud Director and the vCloud api.

I would be happier if they would allow us to schedule sessions as the lines are quite long to get into sessions. Only one session so far today has been full before I got there.

Breakfast was light, I was hungry. Lunch was a little on the light side, and no water? Coffee was good but seems to have disappeared now. Recycling is big this year and that is welcomed.

The conference bag is a nice backpack. My pocket guide took me to the wrong room; I will have to check my conference bag for the bigger book because I didn't see it last night. I'm a winner for CSC's little flyer game. We'll see what I really have won later. I think they have won some contact info :).

VMworld 2010 - Session Full

VMware and VMworld is obviously very successful. It appears

VMworld is suffering from growing pains. With over 17,000 attendees this year, I've experienced the VMworld growing pains first hand. Many of my chosen sessions have been full, leaving me a choice of rushing to another session or taking my chances of eventually getting in. Both are a dice roll, one includes some cardio. Myself and a handful of others end up waiting outside in a line. When one person leaves the session, one of us enters. Today I went with cardio and still ended up in a line twice!

I have seen what appears to be the VMware person who schedules sessions a few times now. This leads me to believe VMware is aware of the overflow of interested people. I have tried to sell my spot in line for $20-$100 with no luck. People seem to think they have paid their due to sit down in a session, I agree.

VMware, we love you. We just really want to hear what you have to say!

VMworld 2010 - vMA

Just attended a session that did a decent overview of the vMA.

MA6580 Bridge the ESX/ESXi Management Gap Using the vSphere Management Assistant (vMA) – Tips & Tricks Included.

With ESX classic no longer something we should be using, we need a way to really manage ESXi. vMA is a VM that you can download from VMware. It is built on centos and contains the vsphere cli as well as the sdk. There is quite a community of people developing scripts for use on it. The VM is also supported by VMware.

From the session there was one site that caught my eye. Virtuallyghetto.com. William Lam has apparently written some excellent scripts for the vMA. A security hardening script and health check script. The session explained the security hardening script has every setting from the security document from VMware.

vMA 4.1 was recently release and you can update to this later version from inside your vMA 4.0 using vima-update. You'll need to use sudo of course.

vMA can assist you with collecting logs from your ESXi hosts.

Here are some vMA best practices collected from the session.
1. Put vMA on a management network.
2. Use static IP and FQDN and DNS.
3. Enabled NTP using UTC, ESXi only uses UTC.
4. Use vMA to connect to vCLI.
5. Limit use of resxtop, resxtop should be used for real time troubleshooting not monitoring.
6. Cleanup local accounts left behind when using new vMA or destroying it.

I will have to make sure my co-workers look over the slides once they are available.

Tivoli 6.x and VMware API for Data Protection

I've been researching Tivoli Storage Manager a bit lately and have some good information to report. VMware API for Data Protection, or VADP for short, is VMware's replacement for VCB. In some ways this is completely new and in others it is going to be very familiar.

You must still use a proxy both ways. For full images you use a hardware proxy and vcb. For file level you can use a Windows Virtual Machine with the 6.2.1 client to backup other Windows VM's. The last row in this table is incredibly vague in all honesty. http://www-01.ibm.com/support/docview.wss?uid=swg21426059.

If you are only interested in file level backups of your VM's, you will likely be happy with TSM's integration to date with VADP. You'll want the 6.2.1 windows client loaded on a windows VM. I used Windows 2008 R2. In this proxy machine you must do some configurations. You cannot use the GUI to do the actual backup. The backup has to be ran just like VCB "dsmc backup vm". At this point in vCenter you should see a snapshot made for the machine you are backing up. You also will soon see the proxy machine reconfigured with that machines vmdk mounted. To see some of the configs in the GUI open the 6.2.1 GUI (i'm using windows). Click on Edit, client preferences, VM backup. You will see on the right where you point it to virtual center. List VM's to backup and select the style. Once this is done you can operate this new proxy VM just as you did your VCB box. Some nice features are backup all windows VM's and then the ability to do a minus VM "-vm" to exclude some VM's.

Some missing features are things like auto detecting new VM's and backing them up. The "All-Windows" selection in TSM will catch the new VM's but it will fail to back them up because they do not have a node in the TSM server. Also, your proxy node has not been granted access to back them up in TSM server. I am playing with some ways to script this but hopefully this is already on Tivoli's roadmap.

Now if you want image level backups you are in for a surprise. TSM does not currently support VADP for image level backups. I currently do not do image level backups for production (that's what replication is for I always said). I am now thinking of doing them simply to have another method to protect data.

If you have any issues, please feel free to contact me. I would love to hear how others are using TSM and VADP.

VMware API Data Protection and vAPP

I have been trying to move as much as possible to vApp containers recently. I just like the idea of a vApp, it makes sense.

vApp is basically two or more virtual machines that make up a system or application. Like a web server with PHP that connects back to a MySQL database server. You would put both of these together in a vApp. vApp allows for some more detailed configuration that you may benefit from as much as I have. Start Order is what sold me on vApp. Now I can say out of a group of VM's that I want one to start first and do not start the second until x number of seconds have elapsed or VMware Tools are ready.

This week we moved from VCB to VADP. We have found an issue that we did not expect. VADP and vApp are not supported together. The VADP proxy does not see the virtual machines that are in a vApp. We did go the extra mile and try to backup the vApp itself, as well as individual machines. For now, we will be forced to back our vApp's up using VCB.

VMware ESXi 4.1 Host cannot exit maintenance mode

Status when trying to exit says "Cannot complete login due to an incorrect user name or password." Yes, it says that with the poor spacing as well. To fix this simply disconnect the host, once complete the host will show disconnected. Now you right click the host again and choose to connect the host. You will again see the "cannot complete login due to an incorrect username or password." message. However now you will be prompted to authenticate it. Once you complete this the host will be fine.

CHAPTER 4: 2011, THE YEAR OF CONFERENCES

Windows 2008 R2 WDDM video driver script

Here is a quick script that will change the video driver to the correct one for Windows 2008 R2 running on VMware.

Installing the new driver using this script REBOOTS the machine so be careful. It is less painless than using mouse etc. inside laggy video machine.

You may need to edit some paths in vmwarew2k8video.bat depending on where you put the files.

Included in zip is devcon.exe for x64 machines needed for this to work. You can also download this version of devcon from HERE on Microsoft's site.. You should already use psexec. You can download it from HERE on Microsoft's site as well if not.

Symptoms of having the wrong driver is sluggish mouse/video performance or a black screen. These symptoms are detailed in VMware's KB article.

This is to be used as needed on Windows 2008 R2 X64 VM's already deployed. If you do not have this issue yet, then make sure you update your template to use the correct driver before deploying.

To use simply type the machine name or IP address as the first argument.

Example: vmwarew2k8video.bat myserver

```
: change c:\admin\scripts\batch\ to the folder this file and the folder vmware-w2k8video are in.
: Example   xcopy  "C:\SOME\PATH\vmwarew2k8video"  "\\%1\c$\vmware-w2k8video" /S /V /I
xcopy   "C:\Admin\scripts\batch\vmwarew2k8video"   "\\%1\c$\vmware-w2k8video" /S /V /I
psexec \\%1 c:\vmwarew2k8video\install.bat
```

Enjoy!

EMC World - 2011 - Las Vegas

EMC World 2011 is well underway here in Las Vegas at the Venetian convention center.

I will be posting notes and information I am able to gather and share from the sessions and speakers.

EMC World - 2011 - VNX - What, When, Where?

Some of my notes from this session may be useful for others.

Information vs Data – Information is good. More information means more business. The bad is the cost to store data. Data is information captured. The goal is to always store the information in the most efficient way possible. – I agree with this on some levels but there are other goals that go with this.

The hardware data capacity is not keeping up. HDD density is only going to be 36x in 2020. While Data is going to be 124x. Compute is going to be 103x. So, we need more compute resources and way more hdd's to keep up with data growth over the next 9 years. Oh, and the budget is only going to be 2x.

The 3 dimensions of storage efficiency is simplicity, efficiency and performance. I've experienced the issue of looking only at $ per GB and GB per sqft etc. Performance then came around to be the most important. $ per io, io per sqft, etc etc. While maintaining a good position of the 3 dimensions.

The first stage in the journey to the cloud is Simplicity. Number of VM's growing quickly. Just now starting VM deployments.
The second stage is large volume of tier 3 VM's. Utility type stuff over in the efficiency area.
The 3rd stage is performance when we put the tier 1 in. Cost is the last thing we should worry about because best performance is what is needed. This is where we were in 2010.

The next generation unified storage is VNX and VNXe. The big boy is the 7500. The smallest is the VNXe3100. – My initial information on VNX makes it sound like it solves all my NS-960 woes.

The where's waldo slide fits us perfectly. We play the 3-card monte with storage. Where's the bits where's the bits. The bits are here the bits are there. Where's the bits where's the bits. Constantly moving stuff around to make the pieces fall into place. Capacity optimization!

By 2012, 80% of all storage capacity sold will be for file-based data. If I keep assigning storage to Celerra like I have been then I agree. Most of our data these days is VMWare Datastores and Celerra NFS/CIFS mounts.

Backup storage is roughly 5x-10x production data. I agree with this. We showed that with Recoverpoint and DataDomain and Tivoli we have many xGB for 1 GB.

VM Storage is only 1/1200 of the enterprise data? I disagree with this. Of course, my company is around 99% virtualized. We have about 50% of our data in Datastores and about 50% in NFS/CIFS on Celerra.

As all this data growth occurs IT starts to ask the business "do you need to store that" We should ask "Should we store that like this?".

To reduce production data, compression at file and block level provides 40-50% typical savings. File level dedup typically around 10%. Block level between 20-28%. VNX uses the first 2 types.

CPU to HDD performance gap – CPU improves 100 times every decade – disk speed hasn't. The solution is FLASH.

EMC World 2011 in FiveFingers

Day two of the conference is winding down for me. I have so far been on my EMC World 2011 journey in Vibram Five Fingers Yellow KSO shoes. I've gotten many positive comments on these wild glove-like shoes. I originally purchased them solely for trail running. I decided what better place to put them through their paces in the early days of owning them than right here in Las Vegas at The Venetian convention center.

The miles of walking between sessions, solution pavilion, vLabs, and the hotel have given me various surfaces to experience nearly barefoot. The cushy carpet in the vLab was weird at first, as was the extremely firm surface of the marble near the Blue Man Group. My feet have thoroughly enjoyed being cool and dry in the Las Vegas weather. Typically, all the walking takes its toll, however so far this year I seem to be quite comfortable.

I was a bit worried that the look would be too much. They are, after all, a bright yellow shoe. Worn with blue jeans and a vendor polo they honestly seem to blend in. I was really surprised at just how many people honestly seemed to like them. A few even knew someone else who had a pair.

I planned to go the entire conference with them and at this point I see no reason I will not accomplish this. EMC World 2011 faux barefoot!

EMC World 2011 - Greenplum

I just completed a vLab on Greenplum. Interesting technology, a purpose build appliance around a database engine. Appears to be mostly for data warehouse type storage with large databases that you cannot supply the performance for today using your current methods.

The demo I saw on Monday referenced a use case at Amazon where 16 billion rows needed to be sliced and diced providing useful data to marketing and executives. For instance, you could look at all purchases for the past 5 years where someone bought a DVD player and then did not buy any DVD's in the last 12 months. Then send them an email with some DVD sales or some other DVD related marketing. The wow factors? The results came back in less than a second. The special sauce? 768 GB of cache.

The box is currently sold in 1/4, 1/2, and whole cabinet configurations. It does support some nice features which I will continue to investigate and see if the technology can apply to the challenges my company experiences.

EMC World 2011 - vLab - Ionix Unified Infrastructure Manager

EMC World has ended, and I am on a plane thinking about Ionix UIM. This is a product that appears to be geared towards configuration of vBlock. I'm interested in answering some questions for myself. I am curious if I can automate the provisioning of new blades as they arrive at my location. I am also interested in automating the provisioning of new chassis as they are plugged into my UCS fabric interconnects. I am interested in automating the full provisioning and configuration of ESXi. Tis could help me move along the path of getting out of the server provisioning business.

Currently provisioning a new blade is extremely easy with UCS. I said easy not instant, fast, or man power free. Unpack and slide in sounds great and not worrying after this point sounds great. Minutes to a couple of hours later have VM's start vMotioning to it would be awesome.

Today we must log into UCS and assign a service profile. Then we zone it in the brocade switches and assign a boot LUN in unisphere. Now we boot it and mount an iso to install ESXi. Then we add the rest of the storage to it that is our normal datastores. Assign a host profile that never seems to be perfect and configure the network. Near this point some final tweaks and we have VM's on it. A process that seems to take us a couple of days at best.

I do not think UIM is going to support brocade, but it might. In he help file I saw only mention of MDS. I bet it does support nexus though. I'll get these questions answered soon enough. The lab the product seems simple from a functionality point of view, but it did meet a key piece of strategy to remove manual process and replace with automation. It also appeared to fill a gap in physical capacity reporting in a single pane though not as good as I want. I would love to see integration with capacity iq to show true capacity including virtual capacity.

All in all, UIM is something I plan to look at further.

EMC Clariion CLI Tips for Lun Trespass

Here is an easy way to find your trespassed LUN's on Clariion.

naviseccli -h 10.1.1.161 -getlun trespass

The output is as follows on my test array:
LOGICAL UNIT NUMBER 37

Default Owner: SP A
Current owner: SP B

LOGICAL UNIT NUMBER 25
Default Owner: SP B
Current owner: SP A

You can use this command to trespass a single LUN.

naviseccli -h 10.1.1.161 trespass LUN 37

This will return you to the command prompt when finished. So, run the getlun command again to see if the LUN is still trespassed.

If you have a lot of LUN's to trespass you can use the following command on both storage processor IP's

naviseccli -h 10.1.1.161 trespass mine
naviseccli -h 10.1.1.162 trespass mine

Cisco live 2011 has started

Cisco live has started here in Las Vegas. My hotel has crappy wireless and I am only able to connect at the conference so far. I have been studying hard this morning for CCIE written Routing and Switching. A little scheduling confusion on my end has me taking this at ten this morning instead of tomorrow. I still don't feel I have studied enough. I need a quick break from the books, so I figured I would announce the start and let all of you know I am here. Now it's back to the book!

BRKARC-3471 Cisco NX-OS Software Architecture

Well this was a very interesting session. Roberto Mari gave the presentation. He is the product manager of the line and boy does he know his stuff. I'm always fascinated by the level thought that must go into designing these switches. The high availability design of the OS is amazing. Running Linux and supporting the multiple processors and other hardware has given some nice advantages. Things like being able to watch processes and if a process stops responding they can restart it with a new pid but maintain the state of it before the crash.

The virtualization that NX-OS supports is of great interest to me as well. My company continues to grow, and I can visualize a point at which we will end up with potentially a production, development, test, etc. networks. The ability separates some of these for real tests especially in conjunction with our ability to bring up machines, the actual machine, a clone of a machine in VMware.

I would suggest reviewing this session on your USB stick if you missed it.

BRKNMS-1032 Network Management KPI's and ITIL

Day two here at Networkers, sorry Cisco Live, is well underway. I am in my first session and it is resonating with me! Utilizing ITIL event management, incident management, problem management, and change management to when providing network services has been on the radar for me recently.

I have been thinking about how to fix my "broken" event management. Sure, we notify of issues on the network. The issue is more about the noise from excessive notifications. The solution? Proper event management. Things like creative tickets and managing their resolution properly for events on the network. Squelching the noise to allow us to clearly hear the actual issues. Moving away from blowing up the email on your phone and instead aggregating events and correlating them.

A lot of the slides in this presentation have excellent KPI's provided via charts and graphs. I have been given a lot of ideas of how

I want to be able to view my KPI's with the new CMDB we have been planning to deploy.

If you have too many alerts, less than ideal change management, or a desire to improve your network management systems I would recommend viewing this presentation. If you would like to see how ITIL can quickly apply to the network world you may want to peek at this session as well.

Cisco Cius Self-Paced Lab at Cisco Live

I am creating this post using a Cisco Cius. What better way to put this device to the test than to use it? I have gone through the basics and advanced self-paced labs here in the world of solutions. The basics covered the android OS on cius as well as how to create a video call and some of the other cool features. The call quality looked great, though a little laggy here on the demo floor, which was to be expected.

Using pocketcloud to connect to a windows 2008 r2 desktop works fine as well. Also, a little laggy but I still think that could be solved with enterprise wireless instead of demo booth wireless. I am using a full-size keyboard and mouse connected via usb to the cius phone docking station.

For giggles I'll undock the cius to prove my connection remains to my RDP desktop and complete this post. Looks like I had to reconnect to my session. The software keyboard is a bit difficult to use. However, it looks like I will complete this post just fine.

Very interested to play with this device in my environment, I see some good potentials.

Quick vSphere PowerShell to see total vCenter configured memory

To quickly determine how bad VMWare's vSphere 5's new licensing is going to hit the company wallet I wrote a PowerShell one liner. It needs vSphere PowerShell to function. Once connected to vCenter the first line will show the sum of configured memory in Megabytes.

```
> get-vm | measure-object -property MemoryMB -sum
Count : 518
Average :
Sum : 2171984
Maximum :
Minimum :
Property : MemoryMB
```

Since VMWare's new licensing says that an Enterprise Plus Processor license is good for up to 48 GB you can do some quick math with the numbers to see how many licenses you need. 2171984 / 1024 = 2121.078125 GB. 2121.078125 GB of configured memory is just over 2 TB. 2121.078125 / 48 GB = 44.18 licenses. So, it appears I need 45 processor licenses to run vSphere 5 with my current memory configurations.

This second line I have added a few more switches. These will show you your largest, smallest, and average memory configuration. The average is useful so that you can figure out on average how much a VM costs you from this new licensing view point.

```
> get-vm | measure-object -property MemoryMB -sum -average -maximum -minimum
Count : 518
Average : 4193.0193050193
Sum : 2171984
Maximum : 32768
Minimum : 256
Property : MemoryMB
```

VMWare vSphere Enterprise Plus retails for $3495 and provides you with licensing for 48 GB of memory. The means each GB you configure on a VM roughly costs you $72.81. My average VM using the numbers above costs $298.14 just for the vSphere 5 license.

This new model will prove interesting soon as better understanding of it is developed. It seems to me that management will see that a VM has yet another license cost. This one tied directly to how much memory we configure and usually waste on a VM. Memory increases on a VM that doesn't consume that memory now have a cost associated with them.

This new model seems like it will hurt some of the large memory configuration blade providers that have 2 or 4 procs but support 256 or 512 GB of memory. Their prices just went up from $6,990 and $13,980 to $18,639 and $37279 My Cisco B200-M2 blades will continue to cost me $6,990 since they have 96GB of memory. I am concerned about those new B440 series Cisco blades I was looking at. 4 Procs but 512 GB of memory, $37,279 in vSphere licenses per box? Ouch.

All prices are list. There are other editions of vSphere that are cheaper however I do not use those. vSphere 5 does have a lot of positive new features that I am unsure if I can live without. Storage DRS for instance is something we have been asking for years.

Cisco Live 2011 Wrap up

Cisco Live has officially ended for me slightly early. I am currently on a plane back to Houston and this entry will be posted once I land. Cisco Live is an excellent conference and I am always saddened when it is over. I attended some great sessions this year.

I was able to catch up on new topics in the routing and switching world. I also learned a few more things and talked to an excellent resource on Cisco Quad. I had discussions arounds wireless that were very informative as well as learned about to some new wireless gear that solves a few issues we have in the field. A meeting with the Nexus and MDS teams has proved to be very helpful. I was able to find a couple of vendors that have some solutions to my network connectivity issues in some of our more remote sites. There just are not many times I can get so much accomplished in a week than these conferences.

Now I am sitting on the plane next to Josh Stephens, head geek at SolarWinds, talking about all the SolarWinds software we have. He has given me several tips and pointers. No wireless up here at 35,000+ feet or I would be testing them out. This ability to network with people in my industry has a great deal of value for me. I am happy that the benefits did not end when I left Las Vegas, running into the head geek was a nice bonus.

A fun future ahead of me now. New wireless gear to investigate. Getting closer to a Quad deployment. New vSphere version was released. Passed CCNA Voice to get started on my voice track. CCNP Voice should sit nicely next to my CCNP Routing and Switching and CCDP. I have jokingly said I may collect the whole set!

Still with all this excitement, to see Networkers end this year is bittersweet. I have VMworld 2011 to look forward to I suppose. It's back to Vegas at the end of August baby!

VMworld 2011 predeparture kick off

Well it is time for VMworld again. I'm excited to go this year as I have been doing a lot of VMware in 2011. I have recently purchased VMware Service Manager, VMware Application Discovery Manager, VMware vCenter Operations Enterprise, VMware Configuration Manager for Windows Workstations, Servers, and Linux Servers, as well as EMC Ionix Storage Configuration Advisor and ControlCenter. I'm looking forward to getting all of it implemented of course. But next week I am really interested in the technical deep dives and continuing to watch for strategic information about these products. I am bringing a 2nd employee this year as my department has grown a bit.

Automation and IT Service Management are big interest points for me this year. VMAXe and VPlex integrations and best practices also are in scope for me this year. To top it all off I plan to spend as much time in the hands-on labs as possible.

If you see me out there feel free to chat me up on topics of interest. I still need to find out if there is a bloggers lounge and take care of some last-minute scheduling.

See you there!

VMWare Orchestrator won't start and no logs

I have been working on a new orchestrator server and ran into this issue. Looked for logs and could not find them in the location they should be. Starting the service would fail with a VMWare specific error that I could not see. In the orchestrator console I saw all green lights and no logging level changes seemed to produce me any logs. Finally, I ran the service manually removing the -s and found the java VM could not start because it could not allocate the necessary memory. I checked wrapper.conf and confirmed it only needed 2048MB to initialize and maximum. I checked how much memory I had knowing it was at least 2GB and whoops it was only 1GB. Doh! Changed it to 3GB and powered on the VM for a successful orchestrator install since the service worked great now.

Moral of story? Measure twice, cut once.

VMworld 2011 - VSP2122 vMotion in VMware vSphere 5.0 Architecture, Performance, and Best Practices

A few notes from the session.

1. The iterative memory copy that vMotion does was interesting to hear more about in detail. I think too many people may not quite understand what a vMotion is really doing. I often just explain it as black magic.

2. vSphere 5 interests me, the idea of multiple nics being used for vMotion. I wonder how best to configure this in UCS. Is vMotion traffic more than client traffic?

3. VMotion ID once found can give details about vMotion in the vmkernel log.

Tests appear to show that vMotion on vSphere 5 is faster, 37% drop in time on vSphere 5.

4. vMotion obviously gains tremendous performance on 10GbE.

5. Multiple vMotion NICs and vMotion performance gain in vSphere 5.

6. Configure vMotion NIC's on the same vSwitch.

7. For best vMotion performance place VM swap on SAN.

8. If you use CPU reservations, leave some CPU for the host for vMotion ~30%.

9. Metro vMotion supported in vSphere 5. Doesn't help us VPlex Geo guys.

10. Conclusion? Upgrade to vSphere 5 ASAP if you want faster vmotions.

11. I'm headed to ask about vMotion over asynchronous distances. If not covered by NDA, I will share ��

Good session for vMotion people.

VMworld 2011 - CIM3135
Compliance and Provisioning in
Your Cloud Using VCM

I like vCenter Configuration Manager more and more as I use it. The reporting and control it gives me is much better than my previous product. I am pointing at my Altiris server with the dust on it. Who am I kidding, I virtualized that product when we installed it. The thought of a physical server not running ESXi on it is laughable to me. I am going to sit here and eat my pretzel while we wait for the session to start. I assure you that your wait will be shorter than mine.

See? Let's begin.

1. This session was a little weird because the presenters would interrupt each other and start talking. Odd.
2. VCM integration with vCloud Director looks cool. Auto discovery and understanding of machines with the same name and IP but in different zones.
3. The change detection is tricky for me. I want to monitor everything that could possibly change because of paranoia.
4. Although I do not use it, VCM can provision OS, via pxe boot.
5. Someone agrees that the cloud should include moving the workload back and forth between the public and private cloud.
6. One thing I had not really considered before but I am now, is giving read only access and reports to the server app owners in my org. We keep this info to the server guys right now.

VMworld 2011 - CIM2452 VMware vCenter Operations Technical Deepdive

I recently acquired vCenter Operations enterprise. I have had a PoC done by VMware to ensure it met my requirements of a consolidated view of what is really going on in my converged infrastructure. Although I have some extensive knowledge into vCOps I am very interested in getting an under the covers look at how some of the data is calculated. I am also interested on how best to monitor my operation and what KPI's I should really be looking at. Then I want to learn how best to interpret some of them. Let's see what this session has to offer....

1. Lol first slide says it's not just black magic! I like this session already.
2. With virtualization capacity is now fluid, I agree.

3. Invisible walls, with VM CPU and memory issues may not be resolved by adding more, contention can play a significant role. Proper troubleshooting is required.

4. With vmview you must monitor end users not VM's. I agree here as well as a user may move between virtual desktops. End user experience is important.

5. The key thing for VC OPs to do for me is to take the tons of metrics I have and to present the end calculation to me. Am I green or red?

6. Dynamic threshold analysis uses competing algorithms, meaning the system uses multiple methods to calculate the trend, then checks to see who is right more often and then uses that method. Genius. These are calculated every night.

7. A version change can cause the normal operation of a system to change. Thresholds may not catch this, but trends have a better chance. I liked this idea.

8. Trending noise to determine abnormalities, this is really going to help my environment since we use several tools that are all sending emails for every little thing. We use our brains today to get a feel for the data center health. I declared this a broken model earlier in the year.

9. Alerts should be an indication of a real problem, yes yes yes! Do not alert on every threshold that is reached. Yes please. May I subscribe to your newsletter!

10. Root cause determination in this product is really root metric determination. It isn't telling you what the problem was just what metric that was being monitored was the starting metric of the issue. I.e. We saw disk latency go to 100ms before the app crashed.

11. Workload is demand divided by entitlement.

12. Right-sizing is a concept I always support, but VM admins and I seem to be on the front line of this alone on this.

VMworld 2011 - CIM1644 The path from Lab Manger to vCloud Director

Lab Manager does a great job of providing environments on the fly via self-service. vCloud Director appears to be positioned to provide the same service in a better way.

One of the first slides in this session shows the terminology map between vCloud director and lab manager. I myself need to remember to go and look at this session online and get a copy of that slide.

Lab manager only supports 1 vCenter, but vCloud director supports 25 vCenters today. VCloud director 1.5 supports SQL now which is a nice change.

This session was mostly about SAP's massive lab manager deployment and PoC of vCloud director to be the successor of this. They have their work cut out for them for migrating all their VM's in lab manager to vCloud.

VMworld 2011 - CIM3235 Leveraging VMware vCenter Orchestrator for Your Cloud Deployment and Operations

For the past 2 years I have been trying to get more value out of vCO. It has seemed like vCO was a dead product. Today the room if nearly full, with hundreds of people in this session. I am very happy to see this. I hope there is more content like plugins and workflow libraries available in them communities for vCO.

One of the first slides eludes to vCO being used to connect VMware Service Manager to vCloud. I hope this happens quickly, I really want this type of capability and agility. VCO isn't about replacing the existing management systems. VCO is to be used to automate the manual tasks you perform in those management systems. Having VSM kick off workflows and automatically input the variables needed for the workflow to being is one of my goals at my company, happy it was mentioned here. I am very interested in VMware's management strategy, I think we can expect good things.

One of the slides in this presentation shows VMware's current it infrastructure from a high level. The next slide shows their end to end business application provisioning. I need to make sure to check these 2 slides out further.

Looks like there is a beta plugin for vCO to control F5 BigIP application delivery controllers. Application blueprints is a term we will be hearing more it seems. Finally, it seems we are becoming aware that there is more to delivering an application that just a web server and a database.

VMware has seen 90%+ reduction in time for provisioning VM's, applications, and scaling applications up with moving to cloud and using vCenter Orchestrator. Days and weeks to hours.

Plugins for vCO are being developed and seem to have some focus. Available on the VMware solutions portal. Hopefully a community can be created around these plugins and hopefully workflows that can help customers get a good jumpstart on using these tools. A plugin sdk and certification program is being created. Single stop market place for plugins is currently in beta.

There is a new instructor course for developing workflows. There will be self-paced online training coming late 2011. There is also a book "Automating vCenter 5.0 with vCO" to be released in 2011. There is a blog for vCO with examples and best practices. This is where I saw the UCS plugin in action.

Hopefully VMware develops a virtual appliance for all their software. A vCO appliance is in the works.

Well, let's get started reducing our OpEx by using vCenter Orchestrator.

TEX2923 and TEX1442 are two additional sessions to look at for vCO.

VMworld 2011 - CIM3257 VMware vCenter Chargeback Technical deepdive

VMware vCenter chargeback is a product I use today. I use it for show back for internal IT costs. I am working to get it tuned to the point I can show where the money I spend in CapEx and OpEx is going. I think the holy grail of configuration for it would be balancing the spends vs usage seen, showing that each dollar we spend is either available or consumed resources. I also wish to use vCenter Chargeback to show that I provide a value back to the business. Cost transparency in how I am running the infrastructure is something i have tried to show, and that needs to exist going forward. Chargeback helps greatly with that.

From the session we can gather a few points.
1. A data collector is good for up to 15,000 VM's or 5 vSphere instances.
2. Charge back managers scale out for performance and high availability.
3. Max config is around 35,000 VM's and 10 vCenter servers.
4. I have heard via various conversations that people want API's into chargeback. It looks like that is occurring. Also a SDK is to be released in Q4 2011

I encourage you to visit the chargeback community on VMware.com. I frequently browse them and there is some good info available there.

Chapter 5: 2012, It ends

Windows

I got to play around with Microsoft Windows 8 client with Metro on a few devices. This new OS from Microsoft seems to have a very few improvements over Windows 7. There is new dashboard type interface that appears to be focused on touch devices. In all honesty this seems to be the only improvement of note.

The touch interface is good. The soft keyboard performed well. The interface was easy to navigate and intuitive. I found the use for it to be mostly eye candy though. Anytime you opened a useful application you were taken back over to a Windows 7 feeling desktop. I looked inside regedit and control panel, I found nothing new here. In fact, many things looked exactly like Windows 7.

The lack of finding anything different in the desktop side of Windows 8 has led me to believe that maybe Metro was just a skin on Windows. As I later discovered, Metro is in fact not just a skin on Windows 8. The Internet Explorer appears to run in a separate space on Metro vs. the desktop.

I asked myself, what is the benefit of Windows 8 to the average corporate worker in an office? The answer is nothing. The real benefits are for mobile workers and those who wish to consume Windows 8 with a touch device. I could easily see using an iPad or other touch device to consume a Windows 8 virtual desktop with ease. This of course would depend on the swipe and other touch capabilities working via remote desktop.

There are a few other remote worker beneficial technologies in Windows 8. As I discover their real benefits in the future I am sure we will discuss them. For now, I am anxiously awaiting the release of Windows 8 client for use in the home.

The future of applications in the cloud

I have recently been paying some close attention to what will be needed for the buzzword cloud to come to true fruition. It is that applications will have to be rewritten from the ground up to fit into tomorrow's IT as a Service and cloud. Cloud has been a word that means nothing without an adjective for me for some time. Private, Hybrid, and Public have been some recent ones that help a bit. A few details keep getting missed Workload Mobility, Self Service, and Elasticity. Applications need to be designed to function in all of these areas to have a real future in the cloud.

Many solutions exist for creating your own private cloud infrastructure. On the bottom of the stack you have hardware and virtualization. The operation, capacity, and performance management of this is something that will need to be compatible in both the public and private cloud.

Workload mobility needs to be seamless and non-disruptive. A VM should not require being shut down, moved, and powered back on as it moves between the clouds. An application that is role based and aware of peer roles becoming unavailable could remove some of the need for this. Applications will need to be able to scale out their roles in the cloud so that manual installation and configuration is not needed.

Self Service is more about bringing agility and speed to requests for service. Low hanging fruit of course is services like a test server for some developers or researchers. However, this can be advanced into things like a manager requesting a new virtual desktop for their employee. Self Service enables some things like virtual machine lifecycle and really can provide for better tracking of the reasons we deployed a service.

Elasticity will come when applications are role based and can scale out with no manual input. This should allow for applications to exist on servers in either a private or public cloud. Infrastructure capacity planning could then function such that you only buy capacity as Capex if it meets a watermark of your usage. If you need to burst your capacity that could be done in the public cloud. When the burst is no longer needed your shrink your capacity by only running in the private cloud you paid for.

The key to all of this is applications must change. The cloud providers really need to take on the campaign to have this accomplished. I think the cloud providers need to get a standard around cloud and virtualization first. Of course, time will tell how well this is accomplished. It is looking like the next five to ten years will be interesting to watch as this application transformation unfolds.

Conclusion

It is time for our five-year journey to end. We've seen the beginning of the cloud era through my eyes, solving of several technical problems, and some tips and tricks to help you. I hope you have found this information inspiring or helped you understand something better.

About the Author

Trace McQuaig created The Systems Engineer in 2008. During his career he has worked in Software, Telecommunications, Oil and Gas, and Mining industries. Positions have always been related to Infrastructure and CyberSecurity and range from Operations to Engineering to Architecture. The author currently resides in Houston, Texas with his family. He enjoys anything related to computers and technology. Current hobbies include UAV's & Drones as well as 3d Printing.

www.ingramcontent.com/pod-product-compliance
Lightning Source LLC
Chambersburg PA
CBHW031225050326
40689CB00009B/1484